Bright Idea

Teacher Handbooks

Using Computers Effectively

General editors
Martin Blows and David Wray

Published by Scholastic Publications Ltd,
Marlborough House, Holly Walk,
Leamington Spa, Warwickshire CV32 4LS.

© 1989 Scholastic Publications Ltd

Contributors: David Wray, Martin Blows
(general editors), Winnie Wade, Pauline
Bleach, Alistair Ross, Graeme Bassett, Chris
Robinson, Kevin Jones, Peter Bowcott,
David Spence, Michael Cooper.

Edited by Christine Lee
Sub-edited by Jane Morgan
Photographs by Isabelle Butchinsky
Illustrations by Chris Saunderson
Printed in Great Britain by Ebenezer Baylis,
Worcester.

ISBN 0 590 76017 3

Front and back covers: photographs by
Martyn Chillmaid; designed by Sue Limb.

Contents

Contents

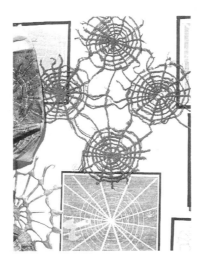

Introduction

The computer has played an increasingly important role in society over the last few years and it is clear that it is very much here to stay. Likewise in the educational sphere, computers are proving an effective and beneficial tool across the curriculum when used with careful planning and forethought.

However, developments in this new technology are taking place at an ever-increasing rate which can be quite bewildering even for the experienced computer-user as well as for the novice. It is hoped that this book will go some way to facilitate the integration of the computer into the primary classroom.

To begin with, let us take a look at the ideal use of computers in a fictional primary school.

A computer-using school

Hightec Primary School has 250 children on the roll, with ten teachers, not including the head. It has children from four to eleven years, and is housed in open-plan accommodation, built in the 1970s. Largely because of help from its active parent-teacher association, it has five BBC computer systems, with a couple of printers and some peripherals such as a turtle and two concept keyboards.

These computer systems are spread through the school, with one being based in each of the five units into which classes are organised. The peripherals are kept centrally and can be borrowed by individual teachers as and when needed. A quick tour of the school will indicate the extent to which the computers have been integrated into its work.

Infant classes

We shall begin in the lower infant unit, where there are two parallel classes of four and five-year-olds. The computer is at present being used in one class area by a group of three children who are engrossed in an adventure game where they have to

Adventure games can be enjoyable and motivating.

help a frog get back home. Several other children keep drifting across to peer over their shoulders to offer advice, and one child keeps saying 'It's our turn next'.

In the adjoining area, three more children are playing on the floor trying to programme a *Big Trak* to steer around an obstacle course of building blocks. On the walls of both areas are several examples of short pieces of writing composed on the computer by the children, with the aid of a concept keyboard.

In the next unit there are two classes of middle and top infants, and the walls here

Word-processed work looks effective when displayed.

have several word-processed stories in their displays. These stories have been written using several different sizes of print. Also on the wall of one class area is a display featuring a large red round figure with a face, and the title 'Podd can . . .'. Underneath are pictures of the figure performing various actions, with the appropriate words written underneath.

The computer is being used in this area by a group of four children who are drawing shapes using a remotely controlled turtle. They have produced several squares and some triangles, and at the moment are trying to get the turtle to draw a house.

A pair of children are going around the area talking to various children and filling in sheets of information about them, for example, their names, their eye colours, what pets they have etc. This information will later be typed into the computer with the help of the teacher, to be used as part of a project on 'Ourselves'.

Transitional classes

The next unit is shared by a transitional class of infants and juniors and a mixed first and second year junior class. The walls of this unit also have word-processed stories on display, and there is one display which features stories which look like newspaper front pages. Also on the wall there are several black and white pictures which have been printed out from the computer. They consist of various combinations of shapes such as squares, triangles, hexagons etc, and all have titles like 'Racing Car'.

Collecting data for a project on 'Ourselves'.

Juniors

In the first and second year junior area, the whole class is writing a story based on their work earlier in the term on an adventure game about dragons. Lots of related artwork and writing is displayed on the walls.

In the unit the computer is at present being used by two top infant children who are experimenting with the kinds of sounds it can produce. They have a program which lets them choose from a range of sound types, and at present their favourite seems to be a warbling sound. They have worked out how to play some nursery rhyme tunes using this sound.

The next unit has two middle junior classes, and like all the others has displays on its walls involving word-processed stories. In this case the stories are all written in different type-faces: some use Gothic script, some use a script like handwriting, and some even have letters with smiley faces on. In the children's writing folders the same story is often printed out in two or three different fonts.

In one of the classes, most of the writing is linked to the current class topic, 'The Vikings'. This has involved using a computer simulation, and much artwork, map-making, drama etc, has been based on this. There are also computer-produced graphs and pie charts using data about the Vikings. A group of children in this class are using the computer to produce a design for a Viking shield. Their computer is equipped with a hand-held mouse which they are using to draw lines and colour in sections of their design.

In another room, the whole class are sitting in front of the television, on which various teletext pages are being shown. The class are discussing the amounts of time devoted in television schedules to various types of programmes, and are using the teletext information to help them.

In the top junior unit, both classes have been working together on a topic based on a computer simulation about a fox's life. This has involved lots of writing and artwork, but a particular feature has been the production of a regular newspaper on the computer which the children have called *The Foxy Times*. Copies are displayed

Some programs can be used to produce sounds.

around the school. At this particular moment a group of five children are planning, on paper, the design of a branching story about the fox. When they complete it, it will be transferred to the computer for the rest of the children to use.

Three children are working at the computer designing their own teletext pages about their topic. This will form part of a teletext magazine which they hope to have running during the next parents' evening.

Administrative uses

Along the corridor, in the headteacher's room, the headteacher and her secretary are debating ways in which the school might somehow obtain another computer. They have decided it would make more sense for school letters to be word-processed rather than produced on the school typewriter, since correspondence could then be saved from year to year which would save a great deal of secretarial time. The head also wants to have easy access to children's records which are stored on computer disk, instead of having to wait until one of the class computers is free.

The current situation

This picture is not, of course, typical. Most schools do not have the luxury of one computer between two classes. Many would like very much to have more computers, while many others barely use those they do have. The point of the school description was to suggest that there is a myriad of ways in which computers can integrate with, and add to, good primary teaching practice.

Surveys suggest that the majority of schools have not yet integrated the computer fully into their teaching. There does seem to be a concentration on the use of the computer as a teaching device isolated from the rest of the children's experience. The reasons for this situation

The computer should enhance the classroom.

can be debated, but it seems very likely that one important reason is simply that teachers have been given insufficient advice and assistance to enable them to exploit fully the potential of the computer.

The aim of this book

This, then, is the justification for this book. Its aim is to give the needed advice and assistance in a way which is sufficiently practical to be really useful to teachers. In the book we cover issues ranging from school policy, to classroom organisation, to detailed treatment of a range of uses of the computer in the primary classroom. This wide coverage will, we hope, make the book very useful to teachers who know very little about computers but who would like to know enough to use them effectively in their teaching. It will also prove useful to teachers who know a lot about certain aspects of computer use, but would like to extend their knowledge to new areas, and especially to teachers given the task of co-ordinating the use of computers in their schools.

As you read, or dip into the book, you might like to refer back to the description of Hightec Primary School to recall the ways in which any of the uses mentioned might fit into the practical classroom situation. After reading the book you might also, we hope, find yourself in the position of the Hightec headteacher, and actively plot ways in which you might acquire one more useful computer for your school.

Developing a computer policy

Developing a computer policy

INTRODUCTION

There are now very few primary schools that do not have at least one computer, and all the indications are that schools and education authorities are continuing to invest heavily in new technology. This investment includes the technical and training support services that are vital to the effective use of computers in schools.

The availability of computer resources does not, however, mean that they will be used to the pupils' best advantage. The key element will undoubtedly be the school's overall policy for the use of computers.

Identifying effective computer use

The computer can be used in a variety of ways in the primary school, and the first task must be to identify the applications from which children can benefit most.

There is no doubt that computers have, in the past, been used for tasks that could be more easily accomplished by conventional means.

Much of the earliest software for

schools was based on the idea that computers would help children to learn specific facts or concepts. However, this meant that software was often little more than an electronic worksheet, allowing practice of basic skills or providing reinforcement activities. Although sometimes attractive, such software used very little of the machine's in-built power or speed and the tasks were not always matched to the children's own needs. Novelty and fun may catch the attention for a short while but is no replacement for the application of skills in real and meaningful situations.

Fortunately educational software has progressed a long way and a vast range is now available. To make the best use of these new resources requires more than a 'taste and see' approach. A policy must be adopted for the whole school.

The overall philosophy must be to use the computer only where its speed, power, graphics or interactive potential can enhance and improve the quality of the work being undertaken. This will introduce areas which have hitherto been beyond the scope of primary children.

Such a broad statement needs further clarification. In order to provide a starting point more specific aims are necessary.

General aims

- A policy should be designed to introduce children to the way in which computers are used in society. Computers are an everyday part of modern life and, as such, children should be confident in using them and understand the consequences of their use.
- There are a number of skills which children need to develop if they are to make effective use of the computer. These should not be seen in isolation but across the whole curriculum. The most important ones are those concerned with word and data processing.

A child who is able to use a word processor will be able to apply that use not only for writing stories or poems, but also for preparing science reports, re-drafting topic work or ordering ideas for

Computers are an everyday part of modern life.

a talk to other children.

The result of continued assessment and revision of the child's work will be a piece of writing which not only reflects true ability but is presented in an appropriate form.

- The policy should enable children to develop logical thinking, problem solving and control techniques, allowing them to take charge of their learning environment. The interactive nature of software such as Logo means that a child can progress at his own rate, breaking problems down into small manageable steps and building a more structured

Ordering ideas for a talk to other children.

approach to problem solving.

- The modelling power of the computer should be used to simulate environments beyond the normal scope of the classroom. There are many excellent simulation packages and adventure programs which create safe environments where children can explore problems within a group situation in a way that would not be possible within a normal classroom situation.

- The use of specific, and relevant, software or hardware should be matched to the particular needs of an individual or group of children. There is still an important place for subject-specific software which uses the interactive nature of the computer to assist the individual child, or groups of children with a particular aspect of their work.

  Such software might, for example, be used to reinforce the ability to interpret a graph, or to explore symmetry. It could enable children with specific learning problems to master a particular skill in a motivating and non-threatening way. Such software will often require other back-up resources and needs to be used with care and skill if children are to gain the maximum benefit.

- The policy should develop the wider use of computers across the curriculum and enhance work already being undertaken. Teachers might argue that they do not have the time within the curriculum to add yet another subject. However, the computer should not be regarded as a new topic, but should be integrated into the other work of the classroom.

  Word processing must not be seen as the domain of language, or database work solely as a part of mathematics. Until the computer is seen as a tool to be used across the whole curriculum, development will be fragmentary and children will not benefit from its use.

Maths software can, for example, be used to reinforce a child's understanding of graphs.

Advantages and objectives

Some of the benefits of using computers have been touched upon already but a clearer statement will provide criteria for teachers to evaluate current use and decide whether they are making the most effective use of the computer.

Computers provide motivation. Anyone who has used computers with children will know how difficult it is to prise them away from the keyboard, whether they are taking part in a group activity, writing a story or practising a particular skill. The best software creates its own motivation whether it is at the keyboard or researching more information in the school library.

Using computers gives children a sense of achievement especially in the area of word processing where the final result can be a perfect piece of writing. The feedback can also be immediate as there is no need to wait for the teacher.

Children can assess and correct their own work in areas other than word processing. Any good software that puts the child in control of his own learning must be able to do this. Drawing a shape using turtle graphics will be a constant

process of trying something out and then improving it. This is not always easy to achieve in other classroom situations.

Using a computer enables results to be presented in a greater variety of ways. When using a word processor it is simple to alter the layout of a page or select a more appropriate print style. Similarly when using database software, graphs can be drawn and redrawn, scales altered and frequency groupings changed by the child in order to get the most appropriate display of data.

The speed of the computer will help children to become more proficient at handling and retrieving data. Tasks that would take a long time by paper and pencil methods are easily accomplished thus enabling children to maintain their interest in the interpretation of results rather than the mechanics of sorting through information.

Computers allow simulations of experiences that would be impossible to arrange otherwise. Looking for a sunken ship, making an archaeological exploration or fighting an oil slick are not everyday events, but a computer can give children safe experience of the problems and decisions involved.

The use of computers encourages the development of group skills because they are rarely used by one child alone. This encourages children to discuss their work and reach group decisions about the best course of action, or the correct question to ask to obtain the information needed from a database.

These advantages are important but they must be regarded in relation to the overall development of the child and a balance struck. Simulation software must never replace first hand experience whenever it is available. Databases do not make graph drawing skills redundant and word processors do not mean that handwriting is unimportant.

Specific objectives

Once the main objectives and advantages of using the computer have been identified, it becomes possible to look more closely at specific areas, possibly with a view to identifying particular skills or concepts that children should acquire.

A list of objectives will give all teachers a clearer picture of the school's aims as well as ensuring a structured development of the children's skills across the primary years. The overall aims of developing word processing skills, for example, might be identified thus:

- to enable pupils and teacher to redraft work more easily;
- to assist in the development of sequencing skills;
- to encourage children to write for a wider audience;
- to enable all children to produce work of equal presentation;
- to enable children to produce a 'perfect copy' to their own design.

By the time they leave primary school the majority of children should be able to use a word processor to write and print their own work. This will involve the following skills:

- preparing – setting-up the computer ready for word processing;

Handwriting is still an important skill.

- entry of text – cursor control, keyboard familiarity and letter and word correction;
- editing – movement of text and simple searches;
- formatting – margin and page lengths, justification and centring;
- printing – use of printer-orientated software.

Keyboard skills

These objectives could be broken down even further to include particular stages or skills. Keyboard skills might be identified thus:

- selection of writing option from software;
- basic keyboard skills, eg upper and lower case letters, shifted symbols (" % & etc), space bar and RETURN/ENTRY key;
- movement of cursor keys around the screen character by character, word by word, page by page and to the start or finish of text.

The objectives may also help to identify particular pieces of software appropriate to different age ranges and tasks. For example, software such as *Folio* is ideal for younger children, or preparing work for display purposes, but is not suitable for preparing a table of results in science or writing a formal letter.

Using computers across the curriculum

Using information technology across the whole curriculum requires a clear understanding about what can be achieved, and what is and is not possible. This can only be developed when teachers are aware of the most important areas of use and the software available.

However, it would not be realistic, or even desirable, for the school's IT policy document to contain precise details for all subject areas. The policy should outline the general aims and objectives, reasons for including information technology within the curriculum, the overall strategy and the specific skills to be developed. It should also outline the ways in which information technology can be used across the curriculum.

More detailed objectives and software titles should be included in specific curriculum statements. Guidelines for language, mathematics, environmental studies, music, science and technology should all reflect the overall aims of the information technology policy.

Computers for maths

The maths guidelines might, for example, highlight specific areas, and include software which can extend or reinforce work. It might also include the development of problem solving skills such as those arising from the use of turtle graphics and Logo or adventure games. For maximum benefit such work needs to be 'built in' and not left to develop on a piecemeal basis.

This must be the task of the mathematics co-ordinator who should be conversant with the school's maths software and be able to explain how it should be used to enhance the experiences already being provided in mathematics. This will help ensure that software is correctly placed within the school's guidelines and matched to children's ages and abilities.

The maths co-ordinator assesses maths software.

It should also be the maths co-ordinator's responsibility to evaluate any new maths software in the light of the needs of the school. Any subsequent purchase should be made from the money available for mathematics. In this way only software applicable to the school's objectives will be purchased.

Policy documents for project work should include the use of larger simulation software, so that the relevant skills are developed throughout the school, as well as enabling the school to provide full resource material for a particular project.

In planning an ecology project, for example, a teacher might list a set of objectives including the following:
- to develop children's map-reading skills;
- to introduce the concept of cycles and balance in the natural world;
- to explore a particular local environment;
- to investigate pollution;
- to develop the ability to make a reasoned argument;

- to develop an awareness of the hidden effects of man on the environment.

In planning these objectives the teacher might consider, along with many other resources, particular items of software for specific purposes.

Simulations

A large simulation program like *Suburban Fox* could be used to direct children's thinking towards the problems facing animals whose natural territory has been eroded by man, or who find the urban environment on their doorstep. The software is only a small part of such an activity which requires other resources in the form of books, pictures, visits, visitors and models to provide starting points for a wide range of work.

The software might form the central part of the project, or could be used at the start, middle or end of a larger project. The simulation program raises many different issues and starting points for work away from the computer. It also incorporates many cross-curricular skills such as group discussion and decision-making, co-ordinates and map work.

Specific map-reading skills can be

Specific map-reading skills can be developed.

developed using software such as *Micro Map* which can be tailored to provide activities at many levels.

A study of pollution with older children might include the use of a program like *Slick!* which simulates an oil slick at sea and includes work on map references, oil pollution measures, costings, decision making and group work.

Word processors

A word processor can assist children who are trying to formulate ideas to make a reasoned argument (for or against fox hunting, for example). The ability to move text around the screen and to arrange ideas can help them to get a balanced argument in the most effective order.

The word processor might be used to prepare work and headings for displays or folders. Desktop publishing programs might also be used to produce group booklets or newspaper articles.

The exact use of the computer will depend on factors such as the length of the topic, the availability of software and the computer itself. The teacher will need to balance potential uses against such factors in order to make the most effective use of the computer.

Deciding on priorities

There are a number of factors which might be used to determine which areas will be given the highest priorities.

Hardware resources

There will be few, if any, schools with enough computers to enable them to do everything that they would like. As soon as there is one computer between two classes the increased use and expectations of pupils and teachers will create its own demand for one per class.

It is therefore necessary to take the school's current position as the starting point and look realistically at resources before decisions are made about which areas are to be given highest priority. New areas can always be added at a later date when more resources become available.

If there is a work station between two

classes it might be practical to expect every child to acquire basic word processing or data retrieval skills. If there is less provision this will not be practical and other objectives and applications will become important.

Financial implications

There are other financial factors which might also have a bearing on areas to be developed. Before embarking on the use of Prestel type databases or electronic mail schools must identify not only the initial hardware costs but the ongoing ones as well; some of which are difficult to budget for.

Control work will need additional resources.

Electronic mail or Prestel demands not only an extra telephone line and its quarterly rental charge but also the annual or quarterly subscription to the database, the time charges for use of the system and the telephone call charges. All this must be balanced against the importance of the data which can be gained, the skills which can be developed and the communications opened up.

A rural school, for example, might well decide that the potential for the children of building links with schools in other areas or large towns through the use of electronic mail does justify the costs involved. If the priority remains high, other sources of funding could be tackled. Local industry might sponsor the school or the Parents' Association might agree to cover the cost.

In a similar way control work will need other resources such as control boxes which link the computer to models, technical building kits, tools and materials to enable children to design and build their own working models.

Classroom management

As already mentioned, much of the best work with the computer is achieved when it is used as a part of a larger project. If pupils are already engaged in problem-solving activities or active group work then simulation software will be relatively easy to fit into the guidelines for project work. The busy classroom teacher will already be used to children working at different activities at the same time. In this situation the computer will fit easily into the classroom with little extra management. If, however, children are unfamiliar with working as a group without direction from the teacher, it may be necessary to prepare them in advance, before using Logo, for example.

Curriculum needs

Another crucial area which must be examined is the school's objectives in different curricular areas. A close look at these, alongside a list of software currently available within the school, will help teachers to see where the computer can be used with effect within a particular area.

Go back to the initial aim and ask whether the computer is necessary for the activity. Does it add a new dimension? If it can enhance the work you are already undertaking it will be worth considering and will affect your own policy in using the computer across the whole curriculum. If the computer merely replaces an activity which is already being successfully undertaken, then this will not constitute effective use.

Current curriculum developments should now automatically reflect the potential of the computer. This may mean new areas being included which have hitherto been unavailable. The National Curriculum guidelines pinpoint specific uses of the computer across the whole primary age range and this must also be taken into account when deciding upon priorities.

Staff expertise

It is important not to forget the most valuable of all resources, that of the teacher. The policy must build upon existing levels of expertise. Making control technology a key area without staff who are able to see the potential for such work, or able to implement such an objective, is unlikely to be successful.

A policy should enable schools to pinpoint their own staff development needs. Although one or two enthusiastic teachers using the computer in a creative way within their classrooms are worth their weight in gold, there are positive benefits in spending time exploring and discussing software away from the classroom situation, or working with another colleague who already has skills in a particular aspect.

The IT co-ordinator

This person performs a crucial role in developing and implementing the school's policy. It is likely, at least in the immediate future, that the IT co-ordinator will be the one member of staff with a global view of information technology, who will be trying

to keep abreast of developments as they occur.

The co-ordinator may well be responsible for drawing up the details of the policy document once the main aims and objectives have been agreed. This will need constant revision.

The co-ordinator can also do much to ensure that agreed practices and decisions are carried out. Group discussions when planning topic work will help to develop the use of information technology across the whole curriculum as well as helping to disseminate ideas and good practice around the school. If the co-ordinator can be released on a regular basis to assist staff with the use of the computer, this will do much to build confidence and make more effective use of computers.

The IT co-ordinator performs a crucial role.

As new software becomes available, especially non-specific software such as databases and word processors, the co-ordinator will have an important role to play in introducing new packages and helping staff to gain confidence in using them. This might be through school-based in-service work, small meetings or working alongside teachers in their classrooms.

Liaison between schools

Another crucial area is that of liaison between feeder schools. This affects not only the children who are entering the school but also those who are moving on to secondary education. The successful implementation of a school policy will have implications for secondary schools which may be taking children with skills and expertise far greater than expected.

Such liaison will also help to build a bridging policy for software and skills development. Although different hardware resources in different phases do not always make this easy to accomplish there will be greater levels of skill transfer if similar software packages are in use or if later software builds on skills already developed.

Indeed secondary schools may need to review their starting point almost on an annual basis as computer use develops in the primary school.

Good links might enable resources or technical expertise to be shared. The use of the secondary school's computer room or colour printer will not only help to implement the primary school policy but also create closer links and ties with the secondary phase to the mutual benefit of all pupils and staff.

Technical support

Other responsibilities for the co-ordinator fall in the technical area. Good technical support will do much to build staff's confidence in the new technology as well as saving much time in the long run.

Back-up copies should (where possible) be made of all new software coming into school and the originals kept unused, in a safe place. Back-up copies should also be made of documentation where logistics, cost or copyright laws allow.

It is important to check that hardware is in good condition, leads are not frayed or plugs loose. Even the occasional vacuum cleaning of the keyboards and cleaning of screens will help to prolong the life of

Check periodically that software is in working order.

expensive equipment. Printers need adequate supplies of paper, and ribbons should be changed at regular intervals. It is also a good idea to check periodically that software is in good working order, unwanted files are deleted from simulation disks, and documentation and resources are intact.

Organising resources

It may also fall to the co-ordinator to organise the use of hardware throughout the school in relation to the work being undertaken by staff and pupils. This will be easier to arrange once the school's policy is clear.

Initially, use of the computer may need to be timetabled to make the best use of available resources, not in the form of a daily timetable, but rather a longer termly or annual plan within the overall aims of the school's policy.

This may mean a class having a work station for half a term at a time to develop Logo skills, or to use a simulation or adventure program. To balance this, there will be similar times when they do not use the computer at all or have more limited access.

The daily timetable of a class will also mean that there are times when the computer is not being used, while children are doing PE, watching television or out on a visit. These times do not have to be

Computers placed together could be advantageous.

wasted. Children from another class can use the computer, either in the empty class or by moving it elsewhere. Such inter-teacher arrangements are easy to make on a games afternoon, or to allow the use of two or even three computers for a short time.

It is also worth considering where the computers are to be used. In small classrooms it may not be practical to have the computer inside the room. In open-plan schools it might be advantageous to place computers together so that they are accessible to more than one class. This grouping can also help with hardware implications. A printer can easily be shared between two work stations by purchasing a printer sharer at a fraction of the cost of another printer.

For some activities it is not advisable to have children working away from the classroom where the teacher cannot make an input into work without leaving the rest of the class. Other activities, such as the use of a floor turtle, will require an area of floor space which may not be available within the classroom itself.

If resources allow, it may be possible to have an 'unallocated' work station, perhaps in the library where children from any class can go to make use of a word processing or art package. As interest grows, children should be allowed to use computers during playtimes and dinner times in order to complete work.

Organisation, therefore, needs to be flexible, arranged around the aims and needs of the school's information technology policy. Staff, children and parents will soon realise the benefits of this type of organisation.

Purchasing more equipment

The IT policy will also provide a structure for purchasing further hardware, enabling schools to look objectively at their needs. If turtle graphics is important, for example, a floor turtle is essential; word processing demands a printer and art packages require a colour printer.

There is, of course, a chicken and egg dimension to such discussions. Until teachers have realised the positive benefits in using computers in the classroom it will be difficult even to start discussing an IT policy. However, once the interest and enthusiasm is sparked, the problem of hardware resources soon arises. From having one or two under-used work stations, staff will be heard complaining about the lack of computers! At this point an IT policy becomes essential!

Children should be allowed to finish work at playtime if they wish.

A plan for action

The following might provide a useful framework for discussing, formulating and finally implementing your policy.

Evaluating computer use

Start by looking at your current computer practice. Work as a team to assess in which areas computers are being used and what software you are using. Evaluate timetabling of computers, comparing the times you have access to the computer and the time it is actually in use. You may be quite surprised to find that you are not using the times available to you in the most effective way. Try to be honest in doing this, or better still get a colleague to do it for you.

Next look at the type of software you are using. There may be a predominance of word processing or subject-orientated software. This will help you to get a clearer picture of your baseline and the areas of expertise you already have. Try to undertake this in a non-threatening way as there may still be staff who are reluctant to share their anxieties about using computers in the classroom.

Check whether the skills being taught to younger children are being developed at a later age. Are data processing skills being taught to all children, or just a single class in a single year? This may affect the use at a later date.

When you correlate this information you may find that your access to the computer is determining the software you are using or vice-versa. If you only have the computer twice a week for half a morning there will not be the time for the whole class to develop word processing skills or to use a simulation package to its best advantage. The chances are you will be using only subject specific software or using a word processor just to prepare handwritten work for a display.

School curriculum aims

Next, look at your overall school curriculum aims. You may have already identified ways of working, or objectives which will determine your priorities for the use of computers. At the same time discuss and relate these aims to the overall objectives outlined at the start of the chapter.

If, for example, you are fostering an investigational or problem-solving approach to mathematics it might help further that aim to use Logo in a problem-solving environment or to develop the use of mathematical adventure games. If you are developing group work skills or an integrated approach to topic work, then simulations may help to achieve some of these objectives.

The problem may arise in that you can identify such uses for all your curricular aims. At this stage you must make a list of priorities and decide which ones are the most important. Another look at the resource implications already discussed may help to clarify these decisions.

Finally decisions must be made about the short, medium and long term objectives for using computers. It might be useful to allocate time limits to these to create a feeling of the school moving towards specific goals.

The short term objectives (for a term or half year) may involve reorganising the allocation of computer time, a better integration of existing software into schemes of work already in operation or staff training on the various uses of the computer.

Medium term (one to two years) goals will pinpoint the development of existing computer work, and widen it across the whole curriculum, with the possible introduction of specific skills for areas such as word or data processing. They will help to determine the purchase of any new software to achieve these objectives.

This will not necessarily mean the

Simulations can help develop group work skills.

Identify the most relevant software packages.

purchase of large amounts of software. It is important to identify the most relevant word and data processing software packages to be used at various ages through the school. However, after this, unless the school already owns lots of software, it will be better to use a few, well chosen packages to good effect rather than risking superficial knowledge and inappropriate use of a large number of packages. This selective approach should make the best use of both computer and software resources.

It is no longer possible for teachers to regard the use of the computer as optional with the choice of activity of minimal importance. These medium term goals will help teachers to identify those areas which are to become an integral part of the school's curriculum and those which will remain an option for teachers with particular interests or skills.

Developing strategies

The goals will also give staff an opportunity to develop new strategies for the best use of the computer in the classroom.

The longer term goals will help the school to decide on the future purchase of new computers, staff training for the introduction of other areas of computer use, and an evaluation of existing policy guidelines in the light of the new technology. They will also help with the assessment of the progress made towards the effective use of computers across the whole curriculum.

Developing IT

This will, for example, allow for the development of 'technology' within the curriculum, initially without the use of the computer, so that when resources do become available children are already working towards computer control work. The implementation of the National Curriculum will make this an important consideration for schools in the future.

Information technology in the primary years cannot be viewed as a single subject, lesson or period within the timetable, but must be integrated into the work already being done by the school. Teachers must ask themselves if the computer can enhance their pupils' learning and experiences in any way. The trap to avoid is, 'I've got this software, how can I use it?'.

The impact of information technology on the curriculum should not be underestimated. If it is decided to develop Logo throughout a school, time must be made for the work to take place. This will not be an extra subject but will need to be incorporated into the mathematics guidelines for the whole school.

The policy will therefore have far-reaching effects not only on what is taught, but also on how it is taught and the classroom organisation and management.

The whole task may seem daunting at first. There are so many exciting things that could be included. It is important, however, to be realistic. Make a list of your priorities, taking into account your starting point, and get these well established throughout the whole school. More innovative work can still continue with the possibility of a wider implementation at a later date.

In any event technology moves so quickly that the policy will have to be reviewed at very regular intervals.

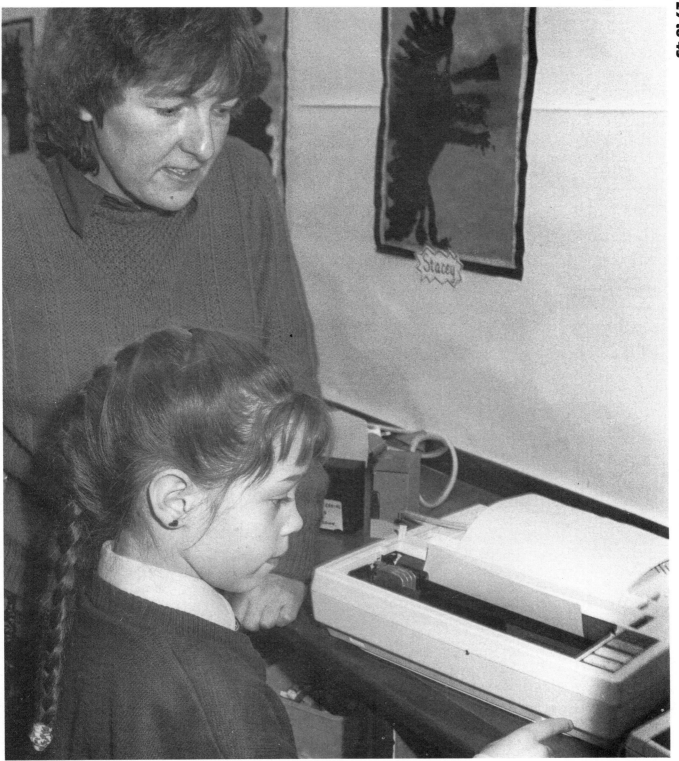

Classroom organisation

Classroom organisation

INTRODUCTION

Any item of equipment in the classroom, be it a workcard or science apparatus, needs to be carefully managed to realise its full potential. Even pencils need careful organisation. Are they readily available? Is the lead the correct type? How can they be sharpened? Despite all its electronic wizardry, the microcomputer is no exception. On the contrary, as a piece of equipment which can be used like a workcard, simulate a siege catapult or be a substitute for the pencil, the microcomputer requires much thought and consideration to integrate it into the primary school classroom.

What are my aims?

The answer to this question is the key to successful use of the microcomputer in the classroom. It is not an answer which can be reached easily, but requires careful thought. There are a number of general aims which all teachers should consider carefully. They include:

- Working towards the computer being accepted as part of the classroom and using it to develop appropriate skills and attitudes.
- Encouraging the children to be aware that the computer is for their use.

- Integrating the computer into the daily activities of the class. It is important to extend the child's concrete first-hand experience.
- Ensuring that the computer is used equally by boys and girls.

Ensure equal use by boys and girls.

Don't just use the computer because it is there: the use of the computer should enhance your teaching and be part of your curriculum. It should encourage active learning rather than passive instruction. It should be appropriate to the individual children in your class and should match their needs.

At this point you need to ask yourself a number of other questions. What do I want the children to learn this year? What topics am I planning to cover? What software will be appropriate for use with these topics? The answers to these questions will identify a number of more specific aims. These include:

- Introducing children to information-handling techniques, eg sorting, classifying, creation and use of a database.
- Developing word processing skills, ie creating and editing text, formatting – margin and page length, centring, using the printer.
- Developing skills across the curriculum, eg maths and language, as part of ongoing classroom work. Will the software provide activities away from the computer, eg using other resources?
- Introducing problem-solving skills, eg use of Logo and turtle. Are the children being required to question, solve problems, discuss and make decisions?

Once your aims and teaching programme for the term or year have been planned, it is essential to decide on how long and over what periods you will need to use the computer. This information needs to be communicated to the staff member responsible for the resource so that your needs can be catered for.

Develop skills across the curriculum.

Where does it go?

Let's assume that you have only the one computer in your school. A policy needs to be developed to make the most of the facility. The following questions should be addressed:

- Is the computer to be used by all or only some teachers?
- Is a computer area to be designated to which children will come to use the micro?
- Who is going to draw up a timetable of computer use?
- Can the computer be made available to a class for extended periods of time for topic work as well as for regularly timetabled shorter periods?

If the computer is going to be moved around the school it will need a trolley which should be capable of taking the disk drive/cassette recorder, monitor and printer. Trolleys with locking cabinets give added security. Make sure that your trolley fits through all the classroom doorways. Split-level schools will present problems

best overcome by either careful timetabling or choosing a fixed location for the computer.

In the classroom there are a number of factors which need to be taken into consideration.

- Are there sufficient power points? You could need up to four sockets. Pay particular attention to electrical safety; do not have any trailing electric cabling which children might trip over.
- Position the screen to avoid reflection from windows and lighting.
- Movement to and from the computer should cause minimum disturbance.
- Position the computer to ensure that the teacher has an overview of the activity.
- Make sure that the children not using the computer are not disturbed by noise; with some computers you can turn the sound off by keying in a simple command.
- Position the monitor so that the screen does not distract the children not using

the computer.

- Allocate appropriate space for such applications as turtle graphics which requires ground area for the floor turtle.

If the computer is to be based permanently in one area, this should be within easy reach of the classrooms. The main drawback in this situation is the difficulty of supervising children using the facility.

The school may well have more than one computer or may acquire more computers as time goes by. As facilities develop, the school policy needs to be reconsidered: a computer each for the ground and first floors? A computer in the classroom of each teacher who makes extensive use of the facility?

The most satisfactory arrangement would be for each classroom to have its own computer with a special area set aside for its use.

Grouping the children

The microcomputer can be used by the whole class, by a group of children or by the individual child. Each of these situations has its advantages and we need to consider them in more detail.

Use by the whole class

Positioned in front of the whole class, the microcomputer can be used as a blackboard to explain or illustrate material. Used in this way, it can introduce the children to a program which they will be using in small groups, or illustrate the finer points of a simulation which the teacher wishes to emphasise. At the end of an exercise, it can be useful to discuss the results with the whole class. The teacher is very much in control and will need to give thought to the size and positioning of the screen. If this application of the micro has been planned into the day's work, try to use a large screen so that all the class can see with ease. Likewise a representation of the keyboard might be important to give clear instructions for operating the program.

Use by a group

Group use represents the most common and, in most instances, the most effective way of using a microcomputer in the classroom. This not only enables a number of children to benefit from the resource at any one time, but also stimulates discussion and interaction within the group. Careful choice of software can capitalise on these advantages, helping the children to improve their reasoning and verbal skills and encouraging social skills such as co-operation, sharing and listening to each other.

Large groups create a risk of exclusion.

Group size

Groups should comprise a maximum of six children, but preferably only two to three. Here are some observations you might consider:
- The number of children in the class and the availability of the computer will determine the size of the group.
- Different programs can be used by different sized groups.
- Younger children work much better in pairs, taking it in turns to operate the keyboard and deciding what to do next.
- Adapt the size of the group to the number of tasks which the software generates.
- More than three children at the keyboard creates a risk of exclusion and discomfort, which in turn can lead to disruption.

Group composition

The composition of the groups needs to be given careful thought, paying special attention to the following points:
- Will you decide on the group composition (ability/friendship), or will you give the children a free choice?
- A group of similar ability usually works well, encouraging lively discussion and involvement for the whole group. For software requiring a lot of reading, a mixed ability group might have advantages.
- The balance of girls and boys in each group. Will you have single sex or mixed groups?
- The personalities of the children.
- Inclusion in each group of a child who is familiar with using the computer.

These considerations will help you to establish the optimal group composition.

Group organisation

Each child must feel that his or her contribution to the activity is important. This can be achieved by allocating tasks to each group member. For example, in a group of three, operating the keyboard, reading aloud from the screen and writing down relevant information are three roles which can be rotated within the group either within one period or over three periods at the computer. These roles will vary according to the nature of the software and will need to be incorporated into the planning process. The favoured role is the operation of the keyboard and this role needs careful management, especially in ensuring that the girls are given equal opportunity. When changing roles within the group, the children will need to change seating positions in front of the computer.

Use by the individual

Although the popular image of computer use is of the individual sitting at the keyboard, this will not be the norm in the primary school. This is not simply due to limited availability of computer time. Most of the current software available is best used by small groups of children involving discussion and collaboration; important activities in the primary classroom.

However, there are certain situations in which individual working is appropriate. Here are some of these uses:

- Some programs are aimed at reinforcing a particular skill and can be used effectively on a one-to-one basis.
- The computer may be used as a means of assisting in remedial work.
- Word processing can lend itself to individual use, for example producing and editing a story or a poem.

Time management

Sharing out a single piece of equipment between several hundred children in a primary school is not an easy task and needs to be discussed thoroughly to develop a clear policy with a positive approach to making the most of the computer. Where the computer time is severely limited, the test of a good policy would be to see how often the computer lies idle. If it sits unused in a classroom, the policy needs attention. If it sits unused in the corridor or store cupboard, the policy needs rewriting.

There are two questions which the

teacher needs to consider, one relating to the time available to the class and the other the time allocation to the individual child.

Class access

'How much time will I have with the computer?' This is a crucial question, particularly if there are only one or two computers in the school. Obviously if you only have the computer for a half day or one day a week, this will prevent you using certain types of software to their maximum potential, eg databases, simulations and adventure programs. In such situations shorter programs which reinforce particular concepts are more appropriate. Ideally each class would have access to a computer for half a term at a time, or certainly for block periods of time. If access to the computer is limited by a timetable, it is important that you make the best use of this time.

Careful long-term planning by all the staff, preferably on an annual basis, makes good sense. This enables you to put your requirements to your colleagues or the member of staff co-ordinating the use of the computer so that a timetable can be produced to optimise the available computer time. If planning a long-term project, negotiate for a greater amount of computer time. This could be achieved by exchanging some of your time with that of a colleague to allow greater access over one term.

Time-sharing is another possibility. Plan work jointly with a teacher of a parallel year group. Although this does not create more computer time per child it does make the computer available for longer continuous periods and enables you to use a larger range of software. Working with a colleague also enables you to share ideas and supporting materials. This can be a particularly good way to build up confidence in using the microcomputer.

Individual access

'How will I regulate the length of time spent by a child or group at the computer?' This depends upon a number of considerations:

- How appropriate to your teaching is the available software?
- What is the type of software being used, eg simulation programs, drill and practice programs?
- What is the length of the task, eg is the word processor being used to write a short poem or a long class newspaper article?
- What are your objectives, eg skill development?
- What other activities are going on in the classroom at the time?

Once your time has been allocated make a list of groups and times so that each group uses the computer in turn. Ask each group to inform the next on the list when they have finished working at the computer.

Make sure that the children's enthusiasm is not dampened by working too strictly to your timetable and do ensure that each group has ample opportunity to benefit from the software. Record-keeping could be of value in assessing your time allocation. Did you leave enough time for group work? Was the software suitable given the time limitations? It is important to make sure that the children regard the computer as a part of the class activities and not as a special treat enjoyed once in a blue moon.

Careful long-term planning makes sense.

Ensuring sexual equality

The counters of the high street computer shops are dominated by boys trying out the latest computer game and improving their computer expertise. Nevertheless computers are equally relevant to males and females and the classroom provides an important opportunity for girls to familiarise themselves with computers and to benefit equally from this tool. This process needs encouragement and there is much that the teacher can do to influence it.

● Evaluate software with girls in mind.

Will both boys and girls enjoy using the program?

● Ensure that the girls as well as the boys can use the computer and associated equipment on their own. Can they load and save data?

● Pay attention to group composition.

● Organise groups so that the girls also experience the keyboard.

An awareness of inequalities creeping in is half way to solving any problems that might arise.

Supervision, observation and record-keeping

All your careful planning and preparation needs to be followed up by supervision and observation of the children working at the computer. Carefully record the progress of individuals as they work through a piece of software or from one program to another.

Supervision

As the class teacher you will need to keep an overview of computer use. Your involvement will probably vary. If the children have never used the computer before they will need help with loading and running programs. The majority of children will be perfectly relaxed and even capable of doing this, probably in marked contrast to your first experience of the computer. The emphasis should be on the care and precautions which need to be taken,

especially with the software.

A class introduction may be appropriate but once the children understand the structure and nature of the program much the same supervision is required as with any other classroom activity. It is important to spend some time with each group asking questions and stimulating discussion about the activity. The skill of teacher intervention needs to be worked at. You must decide whether or not to leave the group to progress by themselves. Be ready to question or make suggestions to guide their thinking.

Once the children have been using the computer on a regular basis they should be able not only to start themselves off but also tidy up and put the equipment away if appropriate.

Experience will dictate what other activities are undertaken in the classroom while the computer is in use. The secret is to ensure that you have time, if necessary, to work with the computer group and that the program does not disturb any class activities.

Observation

It should be clear by now that there is a range of factors which will come into operation when a group of children sit down in front of the computer and begin to use a piece of software. Good planning will lead to a balance within the group and success of the software as an educational activity. Nevertheless continuous observation of each group is very important from the start. Problems which arise are usually concerned with an imbalance within the group, the able child rushing the group through the material, a quiet child failing to express himself.

Be aware of the following potential problems when making such observation:

- An individual child making decisions for the group or telling the others what to do.
- A child spending more than his fair share of time at the keyboard or operating the keyboard too quickly so that other members of the group have not read or understood the instructions.
- A group which is moving mechanically through a piece of software or treating it more as a computer game rather than an educational tool.
- A child who is not making the most of the software through loss of interest, falling out with the group or the other children ignoring him.
- Boys consistently taking the lead role in mixed groups.

Record-keeping

As with the patient recording of other activities in the classroom, you need to decide why you are making a record: for your own information? for the headteacher? or so that you can tell parents how many computer hours their children have

experienced? The nature and detail of the records will vary accordingly. The way in which you make the record will also vary:

- Make a mental note of a child's progress when joining a group: 'Jane obviously enjoyed and benefited from *Granny's Garden'*.
- Use an exercise book or table to note progress or items of software used by individual children:

	Jason W.
Feb.	Granny's Garden
Feb.	Dragon World
March.	Rally A
March	Edword
March	Rally B.

- Set up a system whereby the children record their own progress using either a record book or record sheets located near the computer.
- Set up a system using the computer for either you or the children to store a record of progress or other details. This would only be of value if a printer were available.

Having gone to the trouble of keeping records, make the most of them. Review the software you have been using. Which programs give good value for time? Which children benefit from this mode of learning? How can you improve the use of the computer in your classroom?

Making the most of your computer

Parental help

How do you keep an overview of the computer group, hear the children read and supervise the three or four other group activities going on in your classroom? We all know that the teacher has to have eyes in the back of his head, but managing an integrated day is part of your skill as a classroom teacher. The computer is just another group activity and should not be seen as something out of the ordinary.

Help in the form of parental assistance is available, however, and might be more

necessary with infants than with juniors. Many parents are very keen to help in the classroom. It is quite common, for example, to have parents helping with cookery, art and craft activities or hearing children read. They can be of great support with a computer group, but they must be carefully introduced to the software and understand your teaching aims before being launched into the classroom.

Investing time introducing and explaining the use of the computer to your parent helpers is time well spent. It is important to explain how the computer is used within the school and to dispel any misunderstandings and anxieties which might exist. As with any parental involvement, make sure you are encouraging, thoughtful and well-organised.

Maintenance

The computer is of little use without a monitor, disk drive/tape recorder and disks. You may also have the facility of a printer. This equipment needs to be available and in good working order. The following points should be considered:

- Check the equipment thoroughly before use. If there is a fault, to whom do you go for help?
- The monitor screen collects dust which can be easily wiped off with a cloth.
- Make sure your disk cataloguing system is accessible. You need to know well in advance exactly what software is available.
- A supply of blank formatted disks is essential. These will be used for making back-up material, word processing and saving files from certain pieces of software.
- Is there a sufficient supply of paper in the printer for the work that is to follow?

Associated resources

The computer should be integrated into the work already being done in your classroom. Good software will demand other resources to provide for a wide variety of work away from the computer. These resources could span a number of curriculum areas. For example they may include science and maths equipment, art materials and the associated space in which to use them. They will cover a range of items from books and posters to people. In practical terms you will need to think about availability and storage of such resources. Forward planning is essential:

- What will you need for each piece of software? Don't run out of paper for the printer and find the new pack is stored

Many parents are keen to help in the classroom.

in the headteacher's office (you might find there is a parent visiting, so you'll have to wait!).

- Some software is provided with photocopiable sheets which are essential to the use of the program. Make sure you have done your photocopying in advance so that you do not run out of sheets in the middle of a session. This could be at the very least frustrating, and at worst grind the use of the computer to a halt.
- Introduce worksheets, where necessary, with the whole class before commencing group activities.
- Check that reference books such as atlases are available for the period of your computer-based topic work. Should you put in an order for back-up material from the local education authority teacher support service?
- If the children are going to need access to the resource area or library during their work on the computer, make sure that such space is not double-booked.
- The materials and equipment which the children may need when using the computer should be easily accessible. Colour-coded shelves or storage boxes are a good idea. The children should be informed where they are kept and encouraged to organise for themselves the materials they require and to become as independent as possible.

Computer care

Here are some dos and don'ts to help you look after your machine:

- Keep all food and drink away from the micro; spillages on the computer, printer, monitor or disks will not do them any good! If the children are working at the micro at break time make sure they follow this golden rule.
- Keep all disks in a storage unit (preferably one with a lock). Such units are widely available and are well worth the investment.
- Emphasise the need for care when handling disks – a notice on the lid of your storage unit will help reinforce this.
- Use protective labels on disks to ensure that they are not interfered with or damaged.
- Never leave disks near any source of magnetic field such as the monitor, power supply or speakers (eg television or radio).
- Beware of plugging and unplugging printer leads too frequently as the sockets can be easily damaged. If you only have one printer it is better to keep it attached permanently to one machine.
- Do not allow children to play with plugs and sockets.
- Do not store the computer near the blackboard. Chalk dust can be damaging to both the computer and disks.
- Transportation of computers around the school can be hazardous. A purpose-built trolley which can accommodate a printer as well as micro, disk drive and monitor is strongly recommended.
- Adopt a sensible policy over the security of your equipment. It is not advisable to leave equipment clearly visible in classrooms during out of school hours. If the computer is not fixed at a work station, wheel it into a cupboard and lock it safely away.
- Beware of long extension leads. If these are absolutely necessary, then make sure they are well covered with rubber mats to prevent children tripping over them.
- Fix brightly-coloured notices near the machine explaining how to look after the equipment.

Management and use of software

An early misconception about the microcomputer was that a piece of software could be loaded and the child left to work busily and fruitfully – at last a classroom tool which needs little or no preparation! Under such conditions the computer can be little more than a child-minder. The truth is that effort put into preparing for the use of a piece of software improves the educative value of the program, encourages more work away from the computer and places the machine in its correct perspective.

If sensible use is made of content-free software, you should not feel yourself restricted by the lack of programs available in your school. Content-free software includes word processing, databases, Logo and graphics packages. These programs can be used in different ways many times over – the possibilities are endless.

A number of stages need to be worked through before releasing the class on the next program: they are only too happy to explore the software superficially, much as they would any other computer game which they may use at home.

- Is the software appropriate to your teaching plans for the coming year?
- Familiarise yourself with the software. Do you react well to it? Is it straightforward to use?

Children sometimes view software as just a game.

Find out what software colleagues are using.

- Talk to colleagues who may have used it and see what they made of it. Can you borrow any good ideas?
- Use your local education authority computer co-ordinator to advise you. Look at recent copies of publications such as *Junior Education* for reviews of software.
- Can the software be incorporated into current classroom activities? Can the program be used to stimulate such work?
- Make a list of the information the children require before they begin to use the software.
- Make a list of the skills the children need to master. Do you need a revision session on some aspect of the work?
- Determine the roles the children can assume within their group such as keyboard operation and data recording.

- Determine what equipment will be needed. Is it readily available?
- How are you going to introduce the children to the software? Prepare instruction cards to ensure that the children can use the program on their own.
- Draw up a plan for the use of the software, taking into account other factors such as grouping, time spent at the computer by an individual or group and record-keeping.
- Ensure that any information, instruction sheets or record cards which the children might need are readily available and that the supply will satisfy the demand.

Checkpoints

Finally, here are some of the key points which you should check through before putting your microcomputer to work in your classroom:
- Establish your teaching aims for the coming year.
- Evaluate and decide on appropriate software to fit in with your aims.
- Determine specific times for using the computer.
- Decide on the position of the computer in your classroom.
- Make labels for the computers and associated equipment giving clear instructions for loading programs and the use of the printer.
- Before you use a piece of software read the documentation thoroughly and identify skills and information needed; decide on the resources required; plan the group size and composition and make a class timetable indicating the order of usage.
- Keep a record sheet of the progress and time spent by each child on the computer.
- Enlist parental help if appropriate.

Using word processors

Using word processors

INTRODUCTION

The writing process

Many teachers have been impressed by the way even young children quickly learn how to use word processing programs on the computer and in doing so greatly improve the quality of their writing. What is it that leads to this improvement?

To answer this question we need to look firstly at the ways in which our understanding of the process of writing has changed over the last few years. Perhaps the most significant feature of this change has been the realisation that to expect children to produce well thought out, interesting writing, correctly spelt and punctuated, grammatical and neatly written, at one sitting, is to expect the impossible. Even experienced adult writers do not work that way, and will confirm that any writing other than the most trivial goes through several drafts before it is considered finished. Many teachers have begun to encourage their pupils to approach writing in this way before reaching their final versions.

Why use a word processor?

The use of the word processor as a writing tool reinforces this drafting process. Writing on a computer screen does not have the permanence of writing on paper. Everything about it becomes provisional, and can be altered at the touch of a key, which has very important implications for the way children think and set about their writing.

A significant reason why children may find it difficult to accept the idea of writing as provisional when it is done on paper is the fact that, if they wish to change their writing, this will usually involve re-writing it. The sheer physical effort of this will persuade some children to adopt a much more studied, once-and-for-all approach to their writing. With a word processor, however, alterations can be made on the screen and there is no need to re-write. This allows children to approach writing much more experimentally. They soon become prepared to try things out and alter them several times if need be. They also begin to be able to live with uncertainty. If, for example, they are unsure of particular spellings, they can try an approximation and check it later, without breaking the flow of their writing ideas.

The following two versions of a story written by a six-year-old illustrate this point very well.

Version 1

```
once upon a time there was a baby called
henry and a big dragon too and a boy
called tom and a girl called sarah and the
baby and the dragon took them to the world
of darkness and tom was scared but sarah
said its spooky and scary but the nice
dragons said wheel keep you safe and that
is there best one
```

Version 2

```
Once upon a time there was a baby dragon
called henry and a big dragon called
peter. They had so many adventures but
there best one is when they made friends
with a boy called tom and a girl called
sarah. The baby and the big dragon took
them to the frightening world of darkness
and tom was scared. Sarah said its spooky
and scary but the friendly dragons said
wheel keep you safe and they did. That is
there best adventure.
```

The first version she wrote by herself on paper, and then typed into a word processor. It is a fairly typical infant story with an unadventurous use of words, no punctuation and a plot which seems not to have been thought through. The second version, which she produced after about 20 minutes on the computer, suggests, however, that some of these judgements about her writing ability may have been harsh. Here her range of vocabulary increases, the technical aspects of her writing improve, and her plot, while still not outstanding, at least shows an attempt to take into consideration the needs of a reader. The computer gave her space to experiment, and also to step back from her writing and read it with fresh eyes. These two features are perhaps the most significant of the benefits word processing can give to children's writing.

Resequencing writing

Another significant feature provided by word processing is the facility to cut and paste text electronically, enabling writers to resequence their writing with little effort.

An example of this can be seen in the following story written by two six-year-olds after reading *School with the Troll* by

Elizabeth Walker (Hodder and Stoughton).

```
Once upon a time a troll lived in a bucket
of paint. One day he went to my friends
school and he bit my friends hand and she
shouted miss brown that is her teacher.
Her teacher said go to the head teacher.
My friend is called Sarah. The head
teacher said sit on the prickly mat. Then
it was time to go home and when we went to
bed we heard noises going like this bump
bump bump bump bump and bump. Guess who it
was. You are right it was the troll. He
was green and slimy with red eyes.
```

After discussing their story with their teacher, they agreed that it would improve it if two sentences were moved to different places. This was done with eight key presses on the word processor.

```
Once upon a time a troll lived in a bucket
of paint. He was green and slimy with red
eyes. One day he went to my friend Sarah's
school and he bit my friends hand and she
shouted miss brown that is her teacher.
Her teacher said go to the head teacher.
The head teacher said sit on the prickly
mat. Then it was time to go home and when
we went to bed we heard noises going like
this bump bump bump bump bump and bump.
Guess who it was. You are right it was the
troll.
```

It is, of course, possible to achieve this with pencil and paper by using arrows, or with scissors and adhesive, but neither of these methods compares with the simplicity of the word processor. Again, this facility increases the provisional nature of the writing. Not only can text be changed at will, it can also be rearranged in any number of ways. The full benefits of this will be seen later in this chapter when the area of desk-top publishing is discussed.

Checking details

Most word processors have the facility to search through texts for particular words or markers, and then replace them with other words. This can assist children's writing in a variety of ways. Firstly, it allows them to change their minds easily. If, for example, they have written a story about a boy called Pete and suddenly decide they really want it to be about a girl called Mary, these details can be altered throughout the text by a couple of key presses.

Secondly, it provides a way of dealing easily with consistent misspellings. If, for example, a child regularly spells 'occasion' as 'ocassion', or 'should' as 'sholud', he can be asked to check these words after finishing his writing. Having ascertained

A word processor lets children check their work.

48

the correct spelling, he can then use the word processor to alter every occurrence of the misspelling in one go. Some word processors even allow the user to decide whether such individual occurrence should be altered by pressing 'Y' or 'N' as appropriate. This can be useful if there are words that the child regularly confuses, such as 'there' and 'their', or 'hear' and 'here'. Being asked to consider each one in turn encourages children to become more aware of the contexts in which each one is appropriate.

A further use of the search and replace facility is to eliminate some of the distraction caused when children search for the spellings of words they are unsure of. The words can be entered at first using a marker. When the first draft is done, the children can then find the correct spellings and use the replace facility to change their markers. An example of this can be seen in the following story. The child first wrote:

```
Once upon a time there was a slimy t** who
lived in a paint pot. This t** was f** but
he was only f** with people who were f**
with him. With other people the t** was
fierce.
```

Spellings were then checked, and the replace facility used to produce:

```
Once upon a time there was a slimy troll
who lived in a paint pot. This troll was
friendly but he was only friendly with
people who were friendly with him. With
other people the troll was fierce.
```

Once children understand this technique they can use it to save themselves a great deal of writing effort. Frequently used words can also be entered as markers, and typed once in full at the end of the piece of writing.

Saving and editing

Another important feature of word processing is that writing can be saved on a disk, then re-read and re-edited at a later date. This facility has a very important effect as writing ceases to be a one-shot exercise, with everything having to be right at one sitting. There is, in fact, no limit to the number of times the writer can return to it, and make changes as easily as the first time. Ideas can be considered over a length of time, work can be discussed and new suggestions incorporated, thus making writing a much more thoughtful process.

Allowing children time for reflective editing may initially seem to involve few children having access to the computer for any great length of time. This need not be so, however, because they can print out their writing and take it to work on away from the computer. This can involve crossing sections out, scribbling extra ideas in, and discussing the draft. They can then return to the computer, call up their draft and make any changes they feel necessary, before printing it out again. This process can be repeated as many times as needed.

The idea of using hard copy for revision has another advantage in addition to freeing the computer for others to use. By altering printed text and by crossing out, children will begin to lose their fear of making writing messy. Because of their earlier educational experience, many children approach writing under what has been termed 'the tyranny of the flawless page'. They are extremely reluctant to do anything to disturb this flawlessness. A printout, however, involves very little physical effort and can always be repeated if necessary. This change in children's attitudes has great significance for their future approach towards writing, and helps convince them of its provisional nature.

There is, of course, little point in using a word processor with children unless their work can be printed out. Multiple printouts can be of immense benefit; it is simple to take sufficient copies of a piece of writing for the child to have one to go in a folder, the teacher to have one to display, one to be placed in the child's record portfolio, and one to be taken home to parents. The significance of this is readily seen by considering what happens with non-word processed writing which a teacher wishes to put on display. Often this results in the child having to copy it out, with consequent negative effects on that child's motivation to write.

A further advantage of printed writing is its levelling effect. Many children have poor self-images of themselves as writers, not because they lack ability in the composing aspect, but simply because they find handwriting a strain. In word processing poor handwriting and poor physical co-ordination are no longer a problem and the sense of achievement can be immense. This is not to say, of course, that clear handwriting is no longer necessary. Children still need to be taught handwriting. It does mean, however, that teachers can get beyond the presentation aspects of writing when attempting to make judgements about children's abilities. Most children need help of some kind with their writing, but it is all too easy for teachers to concentrate this help on the physical aspect simply because this is what stands out immediately. If this aspect can be discounted teachers can direct their help to other more important parts of the writing process.

The printed-out text can be decorated for display.

Printing out

Word processed text can be rearranged in various ways on the computer making it possible for children's writing to emerge looking very much like that in 'real' books, with consequent benefits for their motivation to write. The facility to justify text on a word processor helps here. The effects of this can be seen in the following example of the writing of a six-year-old. Her story first looked like this:

```
once there was a dragon called Ace he was

a friendly dragon and Ace met a boy called

john and the dragon said will you have a

fight with me because if you do and you

win I will take you for a ride yes said

John I will have a fight against you John

won the fight and the dragon took John for

a ride to the moon they came back with

straw so they did not hurt themselves.
```

This was then corrected, justified and the line spacing altered to produce this:

```
Once    there  was  a dragon called Ace. He was

a    friendly   dragon.   Ace   met  a  boy  called

John    and    the  dragon said,  will  you  have  a

fight    with    me?   Because  if  you  do  and  you

win    I    will  take  you  for  a  ride.  Yes,  said

John.    I   will   have   a   fight  against  you.

John    won    the    fight   and   the  dragon  took

John   for   a   ride   to   the  moon.  They  came

back   with   straw   so   they   did   not   hurt

themselves.
```

The child was delighted with the presentation of this and commented that it looked just like her reading book.

This ability to rearrange text can be taken further by altering the format of the text. If the writing had been done for a class newspaper, it could be formatted with narrower columns.

Children can use the word processor in pairs.

```
Once    there    was    a    dragon
called    Ace.    He    was    a
friendly    dragon.    Ace met a
boy    called John    and    the
dragon    said,    will    you    have
a   fight    with    me? Because if
you   do   and   you win I will
take    you    for    a    ride.    Yes,
said    John,    I    will    have a
fight    against    you.    John    won
the    fight    and    the    dragon
took    John for a ride to the
moon.    They    came    back with
straw   so    they did not hurt
themselves.
```

Some word processors can print out material in a variety of type styles, or fonts, from Script to Gothic. Such features can enhance children's writing a great deal, and have the effect of making children enjoy writing more.

The teaching device

The word processor can be used as a writing tool for the individual child, but this is an uneconomical use of expensive equipment. Because the writing appears on what looks like a television screen it is much more public than the usual pencil and paper process. It positively invites sharing. A more usual way of using the word processor is for children to write in small groups of two or three. This encourages discussion which will have a beneficial

effect upon the quality of what is produced.

There is also the distancing effect word processors seem to have. They allow children to stand back from their writing and read it with fresh eyes. This enables them to make changes they might not otherwise realise were necessary.

An example of word processors used as a teaching device can be seen in the following piece written jointly by two seven-year-olds. After hunting for minibeasts in the school field, the two boys wrote:

```
today we went out side to look for littel
creatures and we found an ant and one was
red and jamie russ found a big black
spider and daniel jones caught it in his
pot and we also caught a centipede and it
was red and it went very fast and mrs
wilkins caught a earwig and two
caterpillars but one caretpillar escaped
from the yoggat pot and we found some
slugs and they made a slimy trail on the
white paper
```

Their teacher asked them to read the piece, and they were all struck by the over-use of the word 'and'. The teacher used the search and replace facility of the word processor to exchange the 'ands' for markers, and asked them to look at the writing again.

```
today we went out side to look for little

creatures *** we found a ant *** one was

red *** jamie russ found a big black

spider *** daniel jones caught it in his

pot *** we also caught a centipede *** it

was red *** it went very fast *** mrs

wilkins caught a earwig *** two

caterpillars but one caretpillar escaped

from the yoggat pot *** we found some

slugs *** they made a slimy trail on the

white paper
```

This revision produced the following finished article:

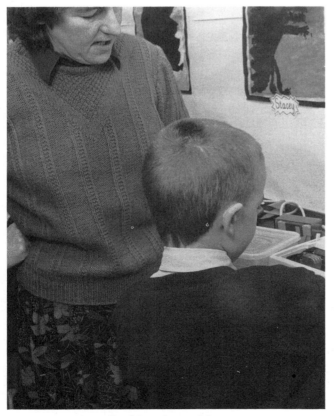

The teacher can offer ideas for revision.

Children will be keen to revise their work.

```
Today we went out side to look for little

creatures and we found ants. One of them

was red. Just then Jamie Russ found a big

black spider. Then daniel jones caught it

in his pot. We also caught a centipede.

The centiped was red like the ant. The

centipede went very fast like the ant. Mrs

Wilkins caught an earwig and two

caterpillars but one escaped from the pot.

Then we found some slugs and they made a

slimy trail on the white paper.
```

The improvement in quality is quite clear. This may have happened without the use of the word processor but it is doubtful if the process would have been so simple, or the children so eager to do it.

There are, therefore, several excellent reasons why word processors should feature prominently in the writing experience of primary children. There are many superb pieces of software available which, properly used, can help achieve the results discussed. Of course, as with any teaching materials, it is the manner of use of this software which is the crucial factor.

Ways of using word processors

The word processor as a typewriter

A common way of using a word processor in the classroom, especially when the teacher and children are new to it, is to dedicate it to producing good copies of children's writing. The children write their pieces in the traditional way, and when these are judged suitable, they are allowed to type them into the computer. Sometimes, for speed, the teacher will assist with this typing.

There are, of course, advantages in this mode of use. Word processed writing is neat and professional looking, typing it in is a reasonably quick task, and the teacher can help things along by taking a turn at the typing, even when the children are not there. Moreover, because not every piece of writing can be typed in, the use of the word processor can be seen as a reward for

children who produce good writing, and this, therefore, gives children an incentive to try harder with their writing.

There are, however, some problems as well. The writing that is typed into the word processor has been considered, maybe revised, and edited before it reaches the computer. The ease of doing exactly these things, though, is the major benefit to be gained from using the word processor. The computer is not, therefore, being used to its best advantage.

Neither is the elitism of this mode of use helpful. If using the word processor is a reward for doing good writing, children who have problems with writing will get insufficient use of the computer for it to help them. And as previously mentioned, it can help them by allowing them space to experiment with their writing. Using the word processor as a typewriter does not encourage this experimentation and so misses the real point of the activity.

The word processor as a composing tool

The word processor is far more beneficial when used as a tool for composition rather than simply transcription. Children use the computer for the whole of the writing process, from the initial jotting down of ideas, to writing a first draft, to revising and editing this draft, to finally printing a finished piece. Of course, using the word processor in this way is very intensive and the group needs a great deal of time in front of the screen. This can be cut down if they

Work can be revised away from the screen.

are encouraged to make regular printouts of their work and take them away to discuss and revise, but there will be occasions when children need to reflect while looking at their writing on the computer screen, to try things out and consider the results, and to talk about what they are doing as they are doing it. Because of these demands upon time, it makes sense to involve children in writing in groups rather than as individuals. This has positive benefits in that it ensures children will discuss their writing, with consequent improvements in quality.

54

Inputting in alternative ways

Many teachers find that it is the actual typing in of text which really takes up the time. Children can be so slow at entering their texts that the frustration is often unbearable for the teacher. It is hardly surprising that teachers occasionally take over the typing, just to speed things up!

The only real solution to this problem is practice. Children *do* improve at typing if they work at it, although with limited access to the computer, this will take some time.

Concept keyboard

There are several alternatives to the keyboard for text input and the most successful of these is the concept keyboard. This is a flat board, connected to the computer, and made up of touch-sensitive squares. Each of these can be programmed to send a message to the computer, a letter, a word, a sentence or a control code, and the computer responds exactly as if this message had been typed in at the keyboard. So that the user knows what is being sent, the messages are written on overlays which are placed on the concept keyboard. As the concept keyboard can duplicate every function of the normal keyboard, many educational programs, not just word processors, have an option for using it. Overlays can even contain pictures, which make the computer accessible to even the youngest of children. Most word processors designed for educational purposes have a concept keyboard option, which will usually allow text to be input from the concept keyboard and also enable the design of new overlays.

There are two ways in which the concept keyboard can be very useful for children's word processing. Because overlays can be made for specific uses, the concept keyboard can be used for child-centred, or subject-centred writing. An overlay can contain words and phrases which a particular child will need. This makes it very useful in a language-experience approach to teaching reading and writing, when it can serve the function of a Breakthrough device. Alternatively the overlay can contain words and phrases relating to a particular topic, which can then easily be incorporated into a child's writing. If, for example, a child is writing about dinosaurs, the overlay can contain the names of several dinosaurs, which will shorten the typing time considerably.

The Quinkey

Another device for text input which some schools have found useful is the Quinkey, although this is not as readily available as it was. The Quinkey is a hand-held box with six keys arranged roughly in the shape of the fingers on a hand. Pressing these keys in various patterns results in letters being sent to the computer, again as an alternative to the keyboard. Initially this device seems very complex, but research suggests that infant children can learn to use it to type in their writing very quickly. A further advantage is the accompanying software which allows four children to write on one computer at one time, each child having a Quinkey each, and a quarter of a monitor screen.

Alternative outputs

As well as there being alternative ways of inputting text into a word processor, there are also alternative ways of outputting the finished product. The usual way is by means of a printer, and, as mentioned, there are several ways of changing the format, such as using different fonts, type-sizes, and layouts. Word processed text does not, however, always have to be printed on paper. There are at least two alternatives.

Speech synthesis

One involves the use of speech synthesis. This allows a child's writing to be spoken by the computer, which, of course, causes great interest and amusement. Current technology has provided speech synthesis

software quite cheaply, although the quality of speech leaves much to be desired, being dalek-like rather than human. It also tends to make consistent errors, especially in vowel sounds, although this can provide a focus for much interesting discussion with children.

Screen output only

An alternative means of output is to send text to the screen only. Many children will be used to getting information from their television screens via teletext systems, and there are several pieces of software which allow children to prepare their own screens to emulate teletext. They can design and write electronic magazines, or even electronic branching stories. Most software of this nature allows the incorporation of simple graphics with text, and its colourful nature makes it very popular with children.

Desk-top publishing

Over the last few years, there has been a dramatic growth in the use of computer systems for desk-top publishing; that is, the production of books, journals, newspapers etc by writers themselves, without the intermediate stage of specialist typesetting.

The potential of this technology as a

Computer systems are used in publishing.

vehicle for the production of children's work is now being realised by schools. It can provide extra facilities for the output of work on the computer. Several of these facilities have important implications.

The first concerns purpose. An important use of desk-top publishing is in the production of class or school newspapers or magazines. These by their nature are intended for other people to read, and their producers are therefore involved in 'public' writing. This adds a dimension of purpose to writing. The public nature of this writing in turn gives children greater incentive to improve its quality and accuracy. Public writing implies also that an audience has to be taken into account. Children can be alerted to the needs of these audiences, and encouraged to reconsider the form and content of their writing in the light of these needs.

A further feature of the production of newspapers and magazines through desk-top publishing is that these media are generally very familiar to children. They recognise their distinctive features and appreciate the facility that desk-top publishing gives them to emulate these 'real life' features. An important stage in the production of a class newspaper or magazine should be the close study by children of real newspapers. In the course of this study many literacy skills can be taught and practised, from the critical reading of advertisements to the factors influencing the impact of headlines. Children may also be introduced to other features, although they are often much more aware than might be imagined of the importance of the typeface used, the layout or the style of writing demanded in particular formats. One of the benefits of using these packages with children is a sharpening of this awareness.

The desk-top publishing environment has some features which make it particularly useful for realistic writing formats. One of the most important of these, which the more elaborate software packages have, is the cut and paste facility. By using this, sections of pages can be electronically lifted from one place and moved or copied to another. This is an extension of the provisionality of writing mentioned earlier. Anything children produce can always be changed in a number of ways, and they quickly learn to experiment with format.

Another feature which desk-top publishing makes possible is the mixing of text and pictures. Software is now available which enables users to take pictures from video players and cameras, and import these as digitised pictures into the desk-top publishing environment. Once under the control of the computer software, these pictures can be manipulated in various ways: stretched, enlarged, reduced, rotated, reversed, chopped into pieces and overlaid or interspersed with text. This enables users of small personal computers to produce pages which are almost indistinguishable from those of real newspapers.

For schools not yet ready for this sophistication, software is available which

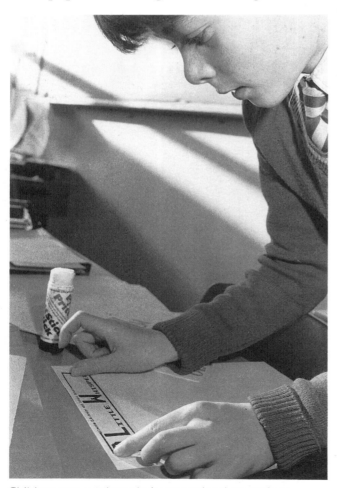

Children can produce their own school magazines.

MOORLAND TIMES 18P

TUESDAY 18 NOVEMBER

LION EATS BOY

PARENTS NIGHTMARE !

On Sunday a boy called Albert Ramsbottem was swallowed up by a lion The Ramsbottoms were very upset as he was their only son.They were upset because it is believed the incident was Alberts fault.It was beleived that Albert Ramsbottom stuck a stick in a lions ear so the lion roared and pulled him in and ate him.The Government reckons we should shoot the lion but the keeper said Wallace is our best gaurd lion.The government says he has one more chance.

Of course this has been no help to the Ramsbottoms.The judge said he hoped they will have other sons, Mrs Ramsbottom said "not likely."

Call for Safe Zoos

Zoos must be made safer the government needs closer bars.

CHILDREN LIKE LION BARS.

Example 1

---

allows children to mix cartoon style pictures with their writing.

The examples of children's work will show some of the potential of desk-top publishing.

The first example is a page prepared by a group of nine-year-olds using a newspaper emulation program. The class had listened to the story of *The Lion and Albert*, by Marriott Edgar (Methuen) and had thought about the story from the point of view of newspaper reporters. The box on the left was left for a subsequent picture to be drawn in. The children's wit is obvious!

The second example was produced by a group of eight-year-olds as an advertisement for the local town-twinning association in which their teacher was involved. The advertisement was subsequently produced *en masse*, and the children were extremely proud to see copies of it in local libraries.

The third example is the first two pages of a much longer story produced by

WOULD YOU LIKE TO VISIT THE SOVIET UNION?

This could be the chance you have been waiting for.The Cardiff/Voroshilovgrad Association will be running a trip to Moscow, Leningrad, and Voroshilovgrad in April.

MOSCOW

Moscow,the capital of old Russia.Home of the Bolshoi.Visit the Kremlin and Red Square.

LENINGRAD

Leningrad, the Venice of the north, is a splendid city of palaces and canals.

VOROSHILOVGRAD

Voroshilovgrad,Cardiff's twin city,is in the Ukraine.The welcome is always warm, and visitors get the chance to meet people and make friends.

DATES:5TH-17TH APRIL 1988.   PRICE:APPROX. £350

For further details contact:
MARY NEWMAN
178 CHAPELWOOD
LLANEDEYRN
CARDIFF

Tel:736171

CARDIFF/VOROSHILOVGRAD ASSOCIATION

Example 2

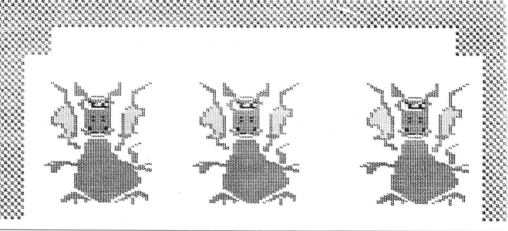

Once upon a time
there was a dragon
called Fred and he
lived in England
with his mother and
father in a cave.

One day he asked his
Mum could he go out
for a fly and his
Mum said yes so he
went to fly.

bye

Example 3

two six-year-olds using a package which allowed the integration of cartoon pictures with writing. In this case the story was written first, and pictures added afterwards to each page. On the computer screen, of course, these pictures were in colour.

These are very simple examples which demonstrate quite clearly the extra dimension that desk-top publishing gives to word processing.

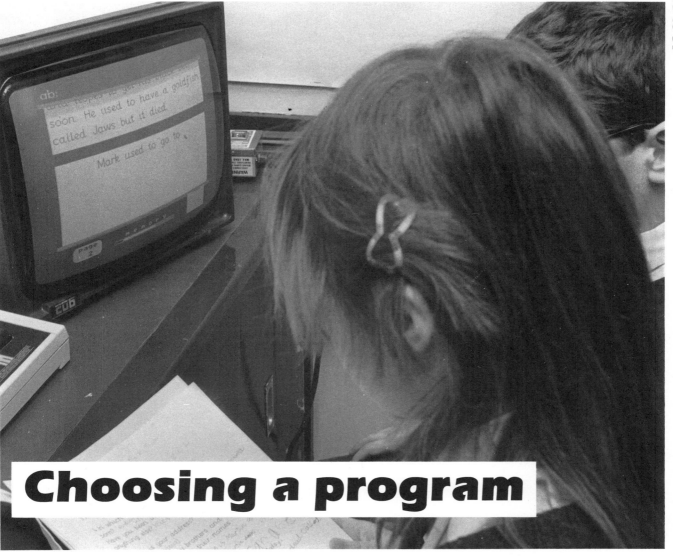

Choosing a program

Choosing the word-processing program for your children can be difficult as there is such a wide range available. The following are some considerations you might bear in mind when choosing. If at all possible, let your children try out a program before committing yourself to it.

Check the facilities available in the program. There is usually a trade-off between facilities and price, but, if possible, the following facilities are desirable:

- insert and overwrite modes;
- cut and paste;
- search and replace;
- control over printout, including fonts used.

Can the program be used with a concept keyboard? The program should have the facility to load in 'overlay files' for individual children.

Does the program have a variety of fonts available, or, at least, does it print on the screen in a font similar to that which children will experience in their early reading books? Can it print on paper using these fonts? This is more important for younger children, but older children can be motivated by printing in, say, Gothic script.

Is the program WYSIWYG? – 'What you see is what you get', which refers to programs in which what is printed out is exactly the same as appears on the screen. Some programs do not do this, and only a few do it entirely. Do you think it matters if children can tell a program to, say, underline a line, or print some words in italics, but do not actually see the results until they get a printout?

Simulations & adventure games

Simulations & adventure games

INTRODUCTION

In the early days of computing in primary schools, microcomputers were used, by and large, to emulate traditional drill and practice routines and were seen to be excellent providers of quick practice exercises. We have come a long way in the intervening years and now recognise that learning, rather than teaching, programs are a much more effective way of using what is often a scarce resource.

One of the major reasons for this change has been the development of more powerful software, such as simulation programs, which enables the emphasis of learning to be on the process of what is happening at the time, rather than on what is achieved as an end-product.

Simulations

A simulation, according to the *Concise Oxford Dictionary*, is something which is made to resemble the real thing but is not genuinely such. A computer simulation is based on a situation, usually real, and is one of the most powerful computer techniques known. This prompts the question of why we should need to use a computer simulation, especially in the present-day climate of learning from first-hand experience. It should be stressed from the outset that no justification exists for using a simulation when real-life experience is available. There is, for example, a maths capacity program which lets children fill up jars from a jug on the screen. This seems a pointless waste of both children's and computer time when so much more could be gleaned from using the actual water measuring equipment.

However, there are three instances when computer simulations provide experience that children cannot get first-hand. These are when the situation itself is too dangerous, time-consuming or costly such as diving to explore the wreck of the *Mary Rose*; searching for the Yeti in the Himalayas or excavating the tombs of the Egyptian kings at Saqqara.

The essence of the simulation demands that children adopt a certain role and either act like the main characters in the simulation or identify with them in some way. From an early age children love to pretend, and simulations provide opportunities to pretend to be, or to act like, something or someone else. There is nearly always the challenge of a problem to solve which in itself stimulates increased motivation to concentrate on the task in hand.

Adventure games

While simulations are usually based upon real-life events, adventure games are not. Adventure games often involve high levels of fantasy and the participants do not generally assume the role of the characters but play in their own right. For instance, in the adventure game *Granny's Garden*, you have to find the six missing children yourself, whereas in the simulation *Suburban Fox* you actually 'become' a fox. In practice, many of the skills developed are the same so they are often discussed together. However, in simulations, small pieces of information are gradually revealed and then acted upon by the participants, whereas in adventure games knowledge is acquired at random, and conjecture and hypothesis determine the route taken through the program.

The skills required and the kind of work produced in both instances overlap. However, in general terms simulations are much better managed as part of an integrated classroom topic whilst adventure

Sometimes practical experience is more relevant than a simulation.

games could be tackled more as independent programs. This, however, would often not achieve the best from them. At the present time, many more simulations exist for the middle to upper junior age range than for younger children. At infant level, though, there are numerous worthwhile adventure games and no teacher wishing to develop this kind of working can use lack of software as an excuse.

Developing skills

The real benefits of using simulations and adventure games can be seen in the kind of skills they develop. We are no longer looking for the sort of results that can be measured easily such as whether a child knows the names and locations of certain towns in America. Instead we are looking for the ability to co-operate with peers, to negotiate, discuss and make decisions. In the simulation program *Wagons West*, children work together, assuming the roles of groups of early American settlers travelling westwards towards California. The development of empathy is one of the main features of this program, but it should be said that much factual knowledge is assimilated incidentally. At the end of using the program, all children will know automatically where Independence and California are, and the nature of the terrain between the two places; more importantly, they will be able to discuss several moral issues quite coherently.

Because we are seeking to educate children for a technological society, it is very important that we furnish them with the appropriate skills. This means moving away from pure acquisition of knowledge to the problem-solving skills of independent learning. One of the best ways of achieving this aim is to use our computers for work which includes adventures and simulations.

Classroom organisation

To organise successful work with simulations and adventure games you don't have to be a computer 'expert' but you do need to be a good organiser. Good computer activity requires that teachers are managers of learning in their classrooms rather than didactic imparters of knowledge. One program which requires this sort of organisation is *Flowers of Crystal*, a creative simulation in which children search to find the six lost parts of the Flower Dream which will put the Flower of Crystal back together. In the handbook for the program, Mike Matson reminds us of what should be the most important point of all in planning our work: 'Please remember that the successful completion of the program should not be the aim. What is important is the activity which results from the use of the program.'

It therefore follows that the best way to ensure an emphasis on the quality of work is to organise the experience as topic or project work. Since *Flowers of Crystal* is designed principally to stimulate creative activities within the classroom, it will make for real cross-curricular work. In this type of work, the software acts as a focal stimulus but a great deal of other activity takes place alongside it. This is illustrated in Figure 1 which shows an example of a topic web demonstrating the nature of integration of various areas of work.

For novices, the teacher's notes provide a step-by-step guide to using the program and give ideas for project work in the various areas. This highlights two further important points. Firstly, be sure to read the documentation fully before attempting to use any software with children. It might be that you can structure the use of the program in a better way than is suggested but it is as well to know what the intended educational aims are. Secondly, it would be rather foolish to try to present children with a program which you had not used yourself first. It is not a very good idea to leave children to get on with it entirely on their

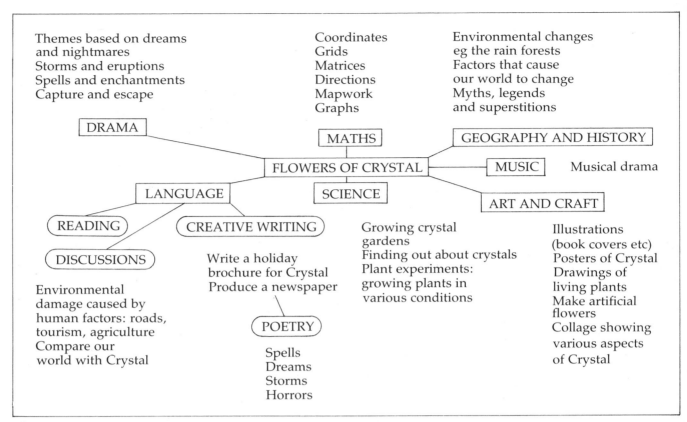

Figure 1

own – difficult simulations require some structured intervention at various stages to avoid frustration. This does not mean that you will supply solutions to the problems but you can provide gentle guidance in the right direction. Of course, good documentation will help you with this but there really is no short cut to this basic requirement.

Resource materials

If the program is to be trouble-free and run well, a lot of time is needed at the planning stage. Besides getting acquainted with the program, you will have to find related resource material. Some software is accompanied by materials such as posters, workcards and even audio tapes, but even so, it is rarely enough. Good documentation will give further sources of information such as specific museums and places to visit. Like any project, a computer simulation or adventure will benefit greatly from a visit either before or during the course of the topic.

Teachers who are new to this kind of work might well like to take a look at the documentation for *Suburban Fox* to see what sort of things are included. In *Suburban Fox*, children take on the role of the fox and have to survive for a number of days despite hazards such as getting caught in a rabbit snare or being run over on a busy road. When we were trying *Suburban Fox* for the first time, a visit to an environmental study centre was arranged to view a fox's earth, but the nearest the children came to seeing a real fox was in a glass case in the museum next door!

Time commitment

Do not imagine that a simulation will just fill up a couple of empty weeks at a slack time in the term. To do it justice really requires a large time commitment. Most of the well-known simulations and adventure games such as *Suburban Fox* or *Dragon World*, will easily take up a whole term. In practice, teachers seldom run out of ideas to broaden and enhance the work; rather they run out of time in which to carry them all out.

A well-prepared simulation is only limited by the bounds of both the teacher's and children's imaginations. Children can become very disappointed if the program has stimulated a new line of enquiry but there is no time to pursue it further. Quite often, too, a lot of preliminary work and discussion needs to take place to set the scene before the actual computer program gets under way.

Starting work

Before beginning a simulation program, you need to consider very carefully where to place the computer. Most experienced users will advocate siting it in the classroom so that it truly becomes part of the everyday working. However, equally good results have been achieved when it has been impossible to move the computer in this way. For example, in one case children had to go out to a central resource area to use the *Suburban Fox* program but the ingenuity of the teacher made each visit seem like an adventure in itself. This was achieved by careful placing of screens and resource materials around the computer to create the effect of entering a fox's earth.

If it is necessary to work in this way, however, teachers should be aware that they are actually losing the opportunity to monitor much of the valuable talk and interaction that occurs. Many of the benefits of using simulations and adventures stem directly from the group interaction and have social as well as educational advantages.

Many questions surround the composition of the groups and though some people will recommend letting the children work in friendship groups, research has shown that a mixture of the sexes, and preferably also of ages, promotes the best results. Children do not naturally choose these kinds of groupings, so again teachers need to be aware of this and lend a 'helpful hand' in making up the groups.

With regard to the size of the groups,

Simulations can be used to inspire imaginative display work.

four seems to work best with younger children while three appears to be more comfortable at top junior level. However, simulations such as *Wagons West* can only work effectively in larger classes if groups of four or more are employed as there are only enough cards for eight individual groups. By the same token, some of the adventure games for younger children can be quite successfully undertaken in pairs, though some of the important skills such as achieving group concensus are missed. Most programs are fairly explicit about the optimum group size to gain the best results.

What to aim for

As with any other work in the classroom, it is necessary to have clearly defined aims and objectives before starting work. It is widely recognised that a good simulation will promote far more work away from the computer than in front of it – the machine only really acts as a catalyst to spark off the rest of the work, so overall integrated activities need to be well thought out. In practice, the computer program usually generates so many ideas that the timing and integration of each aspect need a lot of consideration. If the major outcome of using the program is expected to be an increase in environmental awareness, for example, then the other elements all need to support this.

Let us suppose that we have been carrying out an environmental topic already and that we are aiming to develop children's investigational skills. To support this aim we would select a program such as *Bees* which simulates bee behaviour, allowing children to make their own discoveries about the ways in which bees communicate. The bees forage for food and we can follow their path collecting nectar from flowers and then examine in close-up their dance on their return to the hive. To support the main aim we would have objectives such as these:

- To gain an understanding of the complex communication processes used by bees;
- To appreciate the need in science for

careful observation;

- To adopt a logical and analytical approach to solving problems.

Although the main work with the program will take place in small groups, initially it would be more effective to introduce the idea and concept to the class as a whole by using the computer as an electronic blackboard. How much or how little follow-up work takes place will, of course, depend on the time available but it would be doing a disservice both to the program and the children not to extend the scientific principles generated at the outset. Related activities could include both the transactional and aesthetic aspects of language, art and craft, drama and movement, maths etc. The extent and scope of these will be limited by human factors rather than the extent of the program's stimulus.

Developing aims

The stated aims for a program do not necessarily have to be the ones which are used. In *Wagons West*, which simulates the journey of the early American settlers, the main aim is to develop empathy in the users. The first time we used the program, this aim led to much discussion, and talk and interchange became a major feature of the work. This was in contrast to the type of work evidenced in the next classroom in which it was used where the aim was to use the program as a vehicle for developing information finding skills. Here there was a much larger degree of written work especially in following up suggested contacts by letter. In a subsequent use of the program the aim was to broaden knowledge of other cultures and this resulted in much more art and craft work.

Progression of skills

Whatever the chosen aims, there needs to be a progression of skills. Some software makes this very easy. *Polar Traveller*, for example, for six years upwards, requires simple decision making and logic to avoid

the attendant dangers such as polar bears, snowstorms and floating ice, and acts as an introduction for two other programs.

From seven years, children can move on to *Desert Trek* which involves a Land Rover breakdown whilst crossing the desert. Some direction finding is needed here, and there is more emphasis upon the decision making. In *Jungle Journey*, the scenario is the Amazon jungle with piranhas, cayman alligators, jaguars and snakes. More logical thought is required here and it is recommended for children of eight years upwards.

Two further programs complete the chain. For nine- to ten-year-olds there is *Yeti Expedition* and in *Caving Trip*, the hardest one in the series, the pot-holing experience is based upon the legend of the witch of Wookey Hole caves in Somerset. To solve these you really do need to map out your journey and employ sequential logic skills. These programs are all very easy to start work on and there is a screen of instructions for teachers on classroom use.

Related activities could include art and craft.

Using the programs

Resourceful teachers will be able to find and make back-up materials to ensure that these programs run successfully. Indeed, teachers of all age ranges will be able to effect equally good outcomes by adapting the basic program for use with their own children. For example, *Dragon World*, intended principally for lower juniors, has been used just as successfully with secondary school pupils. If you are stuck for ideas, the resource materials given with *Suburban Fox* provide some excellent models which can be transferred to other, less well-resourced programs.

Assuming roles

Often children will assume particular roles for themselves within the group, such as typist or recorder. Sometimes it is better to leave the children to sort out these turn-taking strategies themselves as part of their group dynamic development, but if you want to ensure that equal opportunities are provided for all members of the group then choose a program such as *Space Programme Alpha*. This simulation for top junior or lower secondary school children suggests that all pupils are members of an Earth-based space programme in which small groups undertake various missions and special assignments. Within each group, roles such as Ship's Captain or Ship's Security Officer are allocated by the computer at random to each pupil. Some decisions have to be made jointly by the group as a whole, while some pre-defined tasks are assigned to particular individuals. This situation prevents children sitting as 'onlookers' in the group.

At the other end of the scale, *Pip Goes to the Moon* for infants ensures that groups get used to taking turns at the computer, since special messages on the screen indicate clearly when each 'go' has finished and when the next group should begin.

Working together

One of the real joys of using most simulations and adventures is that they will encourage co-operative working, often as an incidental to the main aim of the program. *Gold Dust Island*, however, is a program for older juniors which actually sets out to engender co-operation as its main aim. Children using this package soon learn that if they pool their resources and allocate their time wisely on a shared basis, not only are they much more likely to be rescued from the island but they are likely to be a lot wealthier when they leave it!

Software developments

It is easy to believe that if a program has been around for some time then it is no longer of any use, but this just isn't so. Programs such as *Farmer* and *Mallory Manor* are just as effective problem-solving tools today as when they were first produced. Of course, software has improved a great deal in that time and it is particularly motivating to teachers to use a delightful more recent program such as *Cuthbert Catches a Cold* for the lower age range. Developments are such that the computer graphics have been animated in this program to produce an enchanting cartoon disk and a 'Cuthbert's music disk' so that enhanced language work, for example, can continue after children have finished using the main program.

One of the criticisms of some of the early programs was that it could be very frustrating to have to keep returning to the start of a program when trying to work through an adventure. Software writers have learnt from this and users can now choose which section to start from and proceed either sequentially or at random through it. This is known as a menu-driven technique because a list of options is presented to players. It is used to very good effect in *Dread Dragon Droom*, another adventure game for the lower age range. In helping Henry, the little green frog, to rescue the lovely princess Arminda and revert to his former princely self, the user can visit several places in any order or choose to work straight through the adventure along a linear route.

Another recent enlightened development has been to use the concept

keyboard for playing adventure games. In *Rescue*, a fantasy adventure, a glossy, coloured overlay is provided which allows children to progress through the stages by simply pressing the pads. This is especially good for infant and special needs children who can participate without getting sidetracked by difficult typing input.

Nowadays programs can be found to support every area of the curriculum. How much better, for instance, to have a real purpose for understanding the 24 hour clock, than carrying out endless isolated sums. This can also be linked to using timetables, atlases, calculating distances and average speeds in programs such as *Around the World* in which small groups make a journey using various forms of transport from city to city around the world. Once the computer has chosen the specified route, the group must work out its next destination from the clues given, then calculate journey time and decide on an appropriate method of travel, working both from information provided and from other resources.

Bringing the past to life

Simulations are especially good at helping to bring the past alive and many have been written to support historical aspects of the curriculum. One of the most recent of these, for top juniors and lower secondary pupils, is *1665 – The Great Plague of London* which is centred around the Plague and Great Fire of London. It aims to give some idea of what it was like to deal with a major outbreak of plague in seventeenth century London, by assigning each member of the group the role of a Public Health committee member. The first stage gives users some factual information about seventeenth century London so that they are equipped to answer questions such as 'What rules for improving public health would you draw up and enforce?'. A great deal of supporting visual information is given such as the map comparing seventeenth century London with its present environs.

Variations on a theme

Larger simulations all promote cross-curricular topic work by themselves, whereas other packages will contribute to a theme chosen by the teacher. *Red Riding Hood*, for example, is better used to support a wider topic on heritage literature than being confined to its own isolated environment.

Many schools have experimented with the idea of simulating a newspaper office and producing their own class or school newspaper. Programs such as *Front Page* or *Typesetter* contribute to the technical side of this, but there are adventures and simulations available which would help in creating the authentic atmosphere. *Fleet Street Phantom* is a two-part program for lower juniors upwards in which children take on the role of a reporter and visit many departments in a news office to pick up clues and solve the mystery of the phantom who is trying to sabotage the newspaper. This gives scope for the development of many language skills such as finding the missing paragraph which the 'phantom' has torn off an article.

In a similar vein but for slightly older children, *Scoop* is a versatile package which aims to present some of the applications of information technology in an interesting and motivating way. It is concerned with the efforts of a journalist to secure a 'scoop' about the sudden appearance of a millionaire recluse. The user has to keep the computer up to date with current information about the lives of famous people as well as using a range of equipment such as teletext and a fax machine.

For the ultimate realism in news simulations, however, it is much more pertinent to use a program which allows you to present the news piece by piece as it arrives. An example of this type of program is *7 Days in June* for older children. Each of the groups comprising a news team from different papers receive ten short items which appear on the computer display at timed intervals. The children need to employ questioning, connecting, sequencing and empathising in order to handle the evidence appropriately, as well as using their individual creativity.

While this program comes with pre-set data, teachers can also set up this situation for themselves using their own information to present to the children. A piece of content-free software which allows you to do this is *Extra, Extra* which has the added bonus that it can be used with quite young

Newspaper simulations can be put to practical use.

children. Using this as the central resource, work can be linked with other media such as tape recorders, video cameras, Campus 2000, microphones and more traditional resources to allow children the experience of being part of a large newspaper office for a whole day. Naturally, a simulation of this nature takes quite a lot of organising and co-operation between staff but if it is well done, the outcomes are tremendous in terms of personal achievement for the children and in successful development of worthwhile skills.

The outcomes

We are fortunate in primary education in not being rigidly bound by separate subject areas. This means that it is possible to develop worthwhile cross-curricular skills that should equip children for the present-day technological society of which they will become a part.

There is no doubt that effective use of simulations and adventure games contribute in a major way to the development of these skills.

Assessing results

If we are clear at the outset about our aims and objectives for using each program, then it is relatively simple to assess at the end whether they have been reached. Quite often, even if the original aims have not been completely fulfilled, other equally valuable skills and experiences will have been achieved. However, it is only in considering these objectives closely that we will become aware of what has really happened.

Monitoring progress

It follows that some form of monitoring is necessary if we want to be specific about our children's development. Many forms of monitoring are appropriate, ranging from informal observation through to highly specialised response sheets filled in by the children. Workcards and worksheets forming part of the actual program give a good indication of the progression of skills, but one of the most useful devices is to tape record groups of children as they engage in a simulation or adventure and to listen to or transcribe the information later. Even very informal playbacks will offer great insights into the nature of interaction and the level of involvement. One such exercise revealed that even young infant children were unlikely to respond positively to their peers of the opposite sex until they had worked with them for a number of weeks. It also showed over a longer period of study that problem-solving adventure games were a very effective way of developing higher order skills such as decision-making and hypothesising in young children.

A case study

In order to see more clearly what is involved in setting up a simulation or adventure game and monitoring the outcomes, let us look briefly at an actual case study of the adventure program *Robin Hood*.

Scenario

Robin Hood is an adventure game set in Sherwood Forest in the Middle Ages and is designed to be used in the classroom with up to 20 groups of children of eight years upwards. Four of Robin Hood's Merry Men have been taken captive by the Sheriff of Nottingham and are being held in the Upper Bailey of Nottingham Castle. It is the children's task to rescue them and in

carrying this out, they cover four distinct areas centred around the environs of the castle – Sherwood Forest, the Outer Bailey, the Middle Bailey and Upper Bailey.

Educational objectives

The pack gives support for a classroom project of which the computer program forms a part. The documentation states that the program involves problem-solving and decision making; leads to investigative work surrounding Robin Hood and initiates activities relating to the Middle Ages. It is clear that these are specific objectives that dictate the educational outcomes of using this package effectively.

Resource material

The interactive nature of the computer program and the way it is structured will certainly encourage the development of problem-solving and decision-making skills if used as intended. At times children need to try out an idea, reassess their moves and record their progress. Often group concensus needs to be obtained to do this successfully.

Some material is provided in the pack to help with the achievement of the investigative work and the historical background. For example, there is a Castle plan, a black and white booklet on 'Nottingham's Royal Castle' and an A4 colour illustrated book of 'The Tales of Robin Hood'. These proved very useful as a starting point, as did the teacher's notes, but in reality several other resources had to be found to make the project run smoothly. These included information books such as *Castle* by David Macaulay (Collins) and fiction books such as *The White Company* by Sir Arthur Conan Doyle (J Murray). The children themselves wrote for information to The Tower of London Education Service and the English Heritage Education Service. A pre-project visit was made by these Hampshire children to nearby Porchester Castle to set the scene for the topic.

The influence was felt across the curriculum.

Carrying out the project

Once these preparations had been completed, it required minimal teacher time to get the project under way and keep it going. The children enjoyed participating and a wealth of productive activity ensued. It was clear from the start that the computer program stimulated fruitful discussion and that its influence was felt right across the curriculum of these nine, ten and eleven-year-olds. The children worked in mixed ability groups of threes or fours which proved successful, for whilst the reading level of the program material was suitable for all group members, the ability level needed to complete the task was quite high.

Music was also introduced into the project.

It is impossible in such a short space to describe the range of aspects covered and as the project progressed it became apparent that the possibilities were virtually unlimited. It must suffice to give just a few:
- Inside a castle/the castle today/attack/defence;
- Reworking the old ballads and writing new ones;
- Pen-portraits of the main characters;
- Moral issues – could it happen today?
- The Manor Court/feudal system/law;

- Transport/dress/food/housing;
- The morality of theft/unfair taxation;
- Artwork/three-dimensional models;
- Sanitation/medicine;
- Role of the Church;
- Imperial measures/their conversion and complexity;
- The feasibility of forest life.

In the early stages it was useful for the children to be able to interpret maps and it became essential to note relevant information. Some problems could be solved by a trial and error approach such as deducing that no soldier would wear his helmet without his belt while others such as fitting the correct sequence of keys in the three locks required more systematic logic.

Many practical problems were also tackled, such as designing a Robin Hood hat or improving on the audio tape of ballads by adding appropriate sound effects. Making a bow and arrow for the archery competition also proved popular.

The importance of collecting resource materials, preparation and the cross-curricular links was emphasised by the class teacher when he commented that the program on its own would be just a simple game. The children became quite obsessed with the project and spent every spare moment working on the problem both at the keyboard and away from it.

Final outcomes

The most obvious outcome was that the program was successful in achieving its stated objectives. There were also several other beneficial outcomes, many of which can be achieved using any simulation or adventure.

The integral nature of the group work encouraged:
- collaboration;
- co-operation;
- greater confidence;
- turn-taking;
- social interaction;
- self-motivation.

The generated discussion engendered:
- an increase in successful outcomes;
- the development of verbal skills;
- information seeking strategies;
- listening and acting upon information received;
- negotiating techniques;
- positive contradiction and argument;
- providing rationale for ideas;
- the sharing of difficulties and insights;
- the ability to infer and draw conclusions;
- the generation of alternative solutions;
- the ability to discriminate between fact and opinion.

The program tended to encourage worthwhile higher order skills, and in particular:
- empathising;
- reasoning;
- speculation;
- decision-making;
- problem-solving techniques;
- strategy formulation;
- hypothesis forming and testing;
- trial and error approaches;
- short and long term planning;
- the development of logical thought and deduction.

Programs such as *Robin Hood* demand a committed involvement from both teacher and pupils over an extended period of time. Whilst engaging children in a new

Much time was spent away from the computer.

Artwork and modelling were included in the related class work.

independent mode of discovery learning, they also promote a new role for teachers.

Teachers are no longer didactic imparters of knowledge. Instead, they become managers of the children's learning across the whole curriculum. What is most important, is that teachers should identify exactly what they wish to develop when they embark on a cross-curricular package. It is not the ultimate solution which matters so much as the various skills which can be engendered along the way. Often, children will envisage solving the problem as the only criterion that matters, but teachers should be aware that it is the one which matters least.

Data handling

Data handling

INTRODUCTION

'Data handling' may sound rather technical, impersonal and uninteresting, and beyond the scope of primary education. However, many teachers are surprised to find that data handling programs have none of these characteristics, and that their imaginative use can enhance project work and make it educationally more valuable.

This chapter will explain how data handling can help children to:
• solve problems;
• increase their ability to use information;
• think about what kind of information can best help them make sense of their surroundings;
• form and test hypotheses about correlations.

We will look at what sort of information they can collect, and how they can use it to build a database. We will examine how databases can best be designed to allow children to use them as effectively as possible. Several different types of data handling programs will be described, as well as examples of how they can be used. All the examples given in this chapter use the *Dataprobe* software from Longman Group UK Ltd.

Children and information

Children are always collecting information. They spot cars, swap cards and collect information about singers or football teams. In school they may collect data about local history, make traffic surveys and conduct opinion polls.

One of the great problems with collecting any kind of information is that it very soon becomes unmanageable; this is particularly true for young children. Before long, there is such a mass of facts that it becomes difficult to extract anything useful from it, or to make any kind of sense of what it means. This is not a problem unique to primary aged children, of course. It has long been recognised that acquiring information is one thing, but that real knowledge depends not merely on having the information, but upon the ability to extract from it the precise items and details that are needed, and from this, the power to make general statements and conclusions.

This is why one of the most important uses of computers is in the field of data handling: it is also why data handling is one of the most exciting ways in which computers can be used in the curriculum.

A case study

An example of how information handling works in the classroom will illustrate many of these points. Contrast the following two examples of work carried out by third year juniors, one in 1977 without a computer, and the other in 1982 with a micro.

In 1977 my East London class were looking at the local history of the streets around the school. Using the 1871 census records from the local library, we were able to identify families who had lived in particular houses in the street, including some in which children in the class now lived. The census returns were photocopied – each page containing 25 names with details set out in a large table – and mounted on boards for use in the classroom. We had details on 175 local people on these cards: their names, family relationships, ages, occupations and birthplaces. I hoped that by using some simple counting techniques with this material, the children might begin to build up a more generalised view about mid-Victorian life in the area. Groups of children began drawing up tally charts and constructing block graphs to find out the distribution of different trades, the age range of the population, and so on.

There were some problems. Some of these were simply problems of counting. A group would tally the ages on the first card, for example, and then, finding that the second card was being used by another group, move on to the third card – and forget to go back to look at card two. Or playtime would come when they were half-way through card three – and on their return no one in the group could remember how far down the list they had got. The results were therefore inaccurate – not wildly so, but sufficient to make results unrepeatable. Another problem was the laborious nature of the task. Children were willing to go through the data once to try out an idea – but the prospect of testing a further hypothesis by re-examining the information was too daunting. It was difficult to progress further.

The same task – with a new solution

Five years later I was working with another class of the same age in a different part of London. This time we were using a microcomputer and a data handling program with local census returns. As before, we began by looking at the houses today, and then at the records on cards – deciphering examples of handwriting, looking at various details, but at that point not seriously attempting to analyse the information. We then began to consider transferring the information to the microcomputer.

To do this, we had first to construct a data file in which to store the information. A file is a collection of data, held in a standard format, through which the data handling program can sort, edit and extract information. A new file is constructed for each set of information, and can be modified to take in new data or to change

data that has already been entered. The data handling program itself does not hold the information: it is a program that allows you access to all the data files that have been made (Figure 1).

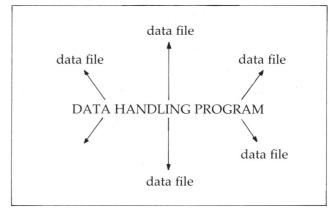

Figure 1

The data handling program can act on a file in several ways:
- create a file (this must be the first step);
- put data into a file;
- amend/edit data in file;
- add more data to a file;
- remove data from a file;
- seek information from a file;
- delete a file (which destroys the data).

Forename	Surname	Address	Age	Sex	Status	Occupation	Birthplace
John	Smith	20 High St	34	M	Married	Silver-smith	Staines
Mary	Smith	20 High St	32	F	Married	Shop assistant	Waterlow
James	Smith	20 High St	7	M	Single	Scholar	Staines
Henry	Smith	20 High St	5	M	Single	-	Hounslow
Lisa	Smith	20 High St	3	F	Single	-	Hounslow

Table 1

Imagine a data file as a large table of information, as in Table 1. Each vertical column is called a field (and the heading of each field is a field name). Each horizontal row, containing the data about a single individual, is called a record. Most data handling programs allow a file to have many fields, often as many as 30, and as many records as the disk will store, perhaps several thousand.

To construct the file, we needed to specify the number of fields we wished to make (we could add more later), and then indicate the name of each field, the number of characters we needed for the data (field length), and whether this data would be numerical or not. Deciding the field length was sometimes a matter of guesswork. We weren't sure of the longest surname, for example, and allowed 15 spaces, while the longest was in fact only 12 characters long. On the other hand, we knew that the sex field would need only one space, for an M or an F. Some other data could be similarly coded, and indeed had already been coded by the original census enumerator.

Building up records

Once the file had been constructed, the data handling program could then be used to enter details about each record. The program would offer a standard format of field names as prompts on the screen, as in Table 2. Details of each record would be entered against the appropriate field name.

```
FILENAME: CENSUS     RECORD NO 1


FORENAME        : ---------------

SURNAME         : ---------------

ADDRESS         : -----------------------

AGE             : --

SEX             : -

STATUS          : -

OCCUPATION      : ---------------

BIRTHPLACE      : ---------------
```

Table 2

Typing in the records may sound quite a laborious task, but shared out between a class of children it was not so. A group of three would sit at the micro: one read out the details, one typed them into the computer, and one checked them on the screen. Each group had about half an hour of this, while the rest of the class got on with other work.

A useful intermediary stage in this process was to make data capture sheets for each record. These were simply duplicated sheets listing each field: the children filled them in manually from the census sheet, checked them, and later entered the details on the micro (Table 3).

```
FILENAME: CENSUS   DATA CAPTURE SHEET

FORENAME        : ---------------

SURNAME         : ---------------

ADDRESS         : -----------------------

AGE             : --

SEX             : -

STATUS          : -

OCCUPATION      : ---------------

BIRTHPLACE      : ---------------

Checked

Entered
```

Table 3

These sheets ensured that time was not lost at the computer deciphering handwriting and gave an opportunity to check the data. The final item provided a useful check that each record had been entered once on the data file.

As the file had more information added, each evening I took a printout of the newly added records to check them for accuracy. Editing mistakes was a very simple task.

One advantage of having all the children share the task of entering data was that they quickly became familiar with the way in which the file was constructed, and with what each field contained. Also, as will be described, knowledge of the raw data gave them some ideas to pursue in making enquiries.

Making a search

When the file was complete, searching the data could begin. The command-driven program we were using required us first of all to indicate that we wanted to make use of a particular file, perhaps ENQUIRE CENSUS. Then we had to indicate exactly what we were interested in. For example, if we wanted to look at the details of women over the age of 50, we would have to check two fields, AGE and SEX. The command for this would be AGE > 50 AND SEX = F. Imagine the large table of information, and running one finger down the AGE column, looking for those greater than 50, and a second finger running down the SEX column looking for the entry F. Only where *both* conditions were fulfilled would the record be selected.

Finally, we had to specify exactly what we wanted to know about these women over 50. If we wished we could have looked at all the information, but some of this was superfluous (we already know their sex, for example). Usually we would want one particular piece of information – perhaps a list of their trades and ages: LIST

OCCUPATION	AGE
-	62
Seamstress	52
Dressmaker	59
Cook	64
-	70
Market stallholder	60
-	63

Table 4

OCCUPATION, AGE. The entire searching and listing processes took less than a minute, searching through several hundred records.

Exactly what one searches for, and asks to be listed, depends on what particular hypothesis is put forward. In Table 4, for example, the hypothesis might have been that in mid-Victorian England in this area women over 50 tended to give no occupation. However, the resulting list would indicate that this hypothesis was not wholly true: some women seemed to have trades. Comparing occupations with ages, one might suggest that there was nevertheless some correlation between age and occupational status. This could be confirmed by making an identical enquiry, but asking for the results to be sorted into age order: SORT AGE as in Table 5.

OCCUPATION	AGE
Seamstress	52
Dressmaker	59
Market stallholder	60
-	62
-	63
Cook	64
-	70

Table 5

Doing this by hand would be tedious: with the micro it is fast and reliable.

More complex enquiries

This example searches two fields, but it is possible to search many more fields at the same time, and in a variety of ways. AGE > 50 AND SEX = F found people who were female *and* over 50 – the word 'AND' *narrowed* the search. Substituting the word 'OR' would *widen* the search, to catch all females, irrespective of age, and men over the age of 50. Thus OCCUPATION = SHOEMAKER OR OCCUPATION = BOOTMAKER will find all boot or shoemakers, instead of having to make two searches.

As well as using symbols such as >, < and =, most data handling programs allow words such as CONTAINS. This can be useful to find records that may contain variations. OCCUPATION CONTAINS SHOE, for example, will find shoemakers, shoemakers' apprentices, shoe repairers and shoe sellers.

In many data-handling programs one can also use parentheses to link together the conditions of enquiries. For example, ENQUIRE AGE (> 40 AND < 50) finds all those between 41 and 49, and ENQUIRE SEX = M AND AGE (> 40 AND < 50) finds males between 41 and 49.

An investigation

Collecting together the data for the data file CENSUS naturally involved my third year juniors in much more than just using the computer. They had already surveyed the street, made a model of it, and looked at old photographs. Thus their investigations into the past using the computer were

Inputting data.

linked to their local knowledge. Creating their own database, as opposed to using one constructed by someone else, gave them more than just knowledge of the kind of information on file, or a familiarity with the structure of the file. It also gave them ideas about what they might look for. 'It

Research away from the computer was also necessary.

seems to me,' said one child, 'that a lot of the young people were born around here, but the older people were born further away.' This observation was to be the starting point for an investigation by a group of children into the origins of the people living in the street in 1871. To test the initial hypothesis, they first divided the population into three groups: those under 21, whom they classified as 'the young'; those over 65 'the old', and those in between. They soon ran into difficulties, because the three categories proved very unequal in size. They decided to find a better way to define their three age categories, and drew a histogram to help them do this. The data-handling program helped here: they made an enquiry to find all records, and asked for a list sorted into age order. It was then a simple matter to run down the list of ages, counting off the number in each five-year age band.

From their histogram they decided on new age limits to the categories – the young were under 18, and the old over 35! They then sorted out each age category, and listed all their birthplaces. Each birthplace was located on a map by a coloured dot, different colours being used for different age groups. The original hypothesis was strikingly borne out. Nearly all the young people were born within five miles of the street, while most of the older group were drawn from the rural counties of England and from Ireland.

The next task was to investigate why this was so. They discovered that the street had only been built in the 1850s, and had evidently been settled in by those migrating to the capital. This led the group to investigate the growth of the railway lines

The computer was used to try out ideas.

that radiated from the city, and the routes that migrants might have taken. Another group of children began investigating origins and destinations, finding not only that people in similar kinds of occupations came from similar regions of England, but also that they tended to settle in similar areas.

All this work sprang from the one initial remark. At each stage the computer offered a fast and reliable way to check out ideas.

This facility to allow hypotheses to be tested is important because it offers children an incentive to generate ideas about correlations between data. If every idea had to be checked out manually, the

task would have been too tedious, repetitious (and probably inaccurate) – all the things that primary education is *not* about! If a smaller collection of data had been used, the results would have been clearly less reliable and significant. But with the data-handling program there was excitement and lively, vigorous enquiry.

Other groups investigated other ideas. Some looked at family size, others at overcrowding, at the distribution of household servants, at the schooling and working life of children. In each case, initial ideas were tested, and fresh ideas generated and tried out. It would have been possible to have kept the class profitably and happily engaged for several months.

File construction

One of the keys to the successful use of data-handling programs lies in the initial construction of the data file. For example, one of the limitations of the CENSUS data file described above is that most of the fields contain data in words, rather than numbers or pictures. Though this closely matches the information in the original census material, we found that it could limit possible enquiries.

For example, birthplaces are given by town and (usually) county. If one wanted to find all of those born in Ireland, the only way to do this with the file above would be to make a search for all the Irish counties – BIRTHC = LIMERICK OR BIRTHC = MEATH OR BIRTHC = CORK etc – which is hardly practicable, and would miss the records where the census enumerator had only recorded the town of birth.

How could numerical data help? We created two additional fields to supplement the information on the place of birth: numerical fields giving the coordinates locating the birthplace on a map. This made it possible to locate an area in mathematical terms. Thus if the two new fields were called BIRTHEAST and BIRTHNORTH, then we could define Ireland on the following map as BIRTHEAST > 550 AND BIRTHEAST < 650 AND BIRTHNORTH > 400 AND BIRTHNORTH < 520 (Figure 2).

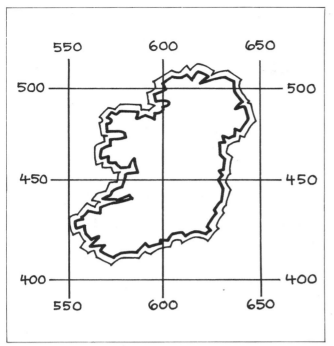

Figure 2

There is a further advantage in using map coordinates with some data-handling programs: it is possible to display results on the screen as a map with the distribution of matching records.

We found that other data could also have numerical codes attached to it. Occupations, for example, were given numbers using a code developed by W A Armstrong, based on Charles Booth's original survey of nineteenth century London. The numbers for similar jobs were closely related, which I simplified further so that the codes for a bootmaker, a shoemaker, a cobbler and a cordwainer (and for apprentices, journeymen and masters in these trades) were all identical. This made searching for particular trades simpler. Furthermore, because related occupations were grouped together, it was possible to locate all those in transport industries, for example, with a command such as TRADECODE (> 300 AND < 400). An enquiry like this would be impossible without coding.

Just as maps can be displayed on the screen with a superimposed distribution, so can other numerical data be presented as histograms, graphs and pie charts in several data-handling programs. Graphic representation presents children with new opportunities to trace correlations and to draw conclusions from data. Of course, children will still need to be able to draw their own graph representations but computer-generated graphs give enormous scope for experimentation and for learning how to interpret data.

Children will need access to other resources for background information.

More kinds of data files

All the examples of data-handling given so far have been based on one data file on the census. Data-handling programs can, of course, deal with a wide variety of files. Younger children often create data files based on themselves and their friends. Again, each record refers to one person, with various fields containing characteristics such as age, height, hair colour and favourite food. Individual children or small groups might compile files based on hobbies and interests such as cars, football teams or characters from stories. In each instance, it is possible for children to search the data that has been compiled to produce interesting and new analyses.

This technique particularly lends itself to class-based projects about the natural environment, local society or scientific experiments. With any of these, it is crucial to plan the construction of the file carefully. In the CENSUS file, each record contained details about one person. But consider the following examples of class projects, all of which I have used with primary aged children:

- a street survey on people's attitudes towards commercial banks;
- the results of a series of experiments to test the strength of conkers;
- the results of experiments with differently designed parachutes;
- a survey of litter, in which children measured the quantity and location of litter and interviewed passers-by on their views;
- a survey of how birds used a bird-table, noting what birds around the table were doing at regular intervals over several days.

The survey of people's opinions on banks, like the census, clearly will have each record based on the responses on one individual. However, in the conker experiments, each conker was measured (weight, volume, etc) before being subjected to a weight being dropped from increasing heights to test strength. In this case, each record was about the characteristics of one conker. The data from the parachute experiment was rather different. The conkers could only be tested once: each parachute was tested several times. It would have been possible to have calculated an average drop time for each parachute, but this would have required continual updating as new tests were undertaken. Therefore in this case, each record was designed to contain information about one single experiment, rather than a particular item.

The litter survey was more complex. Two related types of data were being collected: the views of individuals (related to where the interview took place) and the various densities of particular kinds of rubbish (also related to location). To handle this information properly, two data files were constructed. One recorded the details and opinions of each individual interviewed, and included two fields that gave the coordinates of the location of the interview. The second data file recorded information about each separate location, one record for each square on the grid. In this file, the fields record the density of each particular kind of rubbish – cigarette ends, fast food containers, sweet wrappers, etc. The first data file, based on individuals,

can be used to correlate opinions, and where necessary, to relate these to the actual distribution of litter. The second data file located the actual levels of distribution of litter, by separate areas. They had to be treated separately, but analysing the results could tell us, for example, whether people's opinions about waste paper, etc, were related to the amount of litter around the place where they were interviewed.

The bird table survey also presented complexities. One system would be to record the set of observations made at a particular time. This might require, for example, a data file which listed, as fields, each possible variety of bird, so that numbers could be entered. A record would be of a moment in time, and might look like this:

Month	September
Day	17
Time	14.30 pm
Number	9
Sparrow	4
Blackbird	1
Robin	0
Chaffinch	3
Others	1 Magpie
Temp	17°C
Rain	0.15mm

Bird table visitors could be included in a data file.

Such a file would not allow us to plot the activities of individual birds; what the solitary blackbird was doing, for example. This would need a second file, in which each record contained the details of each individual sighting of a bird. Each data record might look like this:

Time	3.30
Day	22
Month	October
Type	Blackbird
Activity	Feeding in garden
Others	2 Chaffinches, 1 Robin

This file's structure enables children to determine the pattern of behaviour of a particular type of bird.

These examples show that files can be arranged so that records are not necessarily based on one individual or one item. Records can also be the results of experiments, details about a particular location, or details of a moment in time. How the file is constructed will depend on the nature of the information in the project, and the uses to which you think it might be put.

Having decided on what sort of records are going to be collected, consider next what items will be recorded in each field. While it is desirable that children be closely involved in deciding what data to collect, the teacher also needs to think carefully about the potential investigations. As a general rule, it's better to collect too much detail than too little. The construction of questionnaires, for example, requires particular care. As well as collecting answers to questions, it can be very useful to gather data such as the sex and approximate age of the person, and perhaps their occupation. These sorts of item will allow the children to make a whole series of hypotheses about the opinions of different groups. Questions asked also need attention: it's helpful to encourage questions that either have a yes/

Children should be involved in deciding what data to collect.

no answer, or a number answer, or an answer from a short list which can be ticked. These sorts of answers not only make for easily encoded data, but also mean that children aren't left struggling to write down long statements of opinion from passers-by!

Pre-constructed data files

Data files can be constructed by teachers, or can be bought commercially as part of a data-handling program. These save the potential tedium of compiling the records – but they also mean that the direct contact between information collection and data-handling is lost. It is important that children fully understand the nature of the data-entering process and its relationship to making enquiries. They should appreciate that files are made up by people, and that they can be fallible. It is advisable to remember the jargon GIGO, which stands for 'Garbage in, garbage out'. In other words, the information taken out of the data file is only as good as the information entered into it in the first place. Constructing their own file means that children take possession of the data, and feel a sense of ownership.

On the other hand, other people's data files can have some uses. For example,

using the census file one could set a problem like this: imagine that you are an 1871 police officer – armed with a computer, a data-handling program and a file on the census. The following incident is reported (Figure 3):

'At 10.30 pm two young men were observed breaking into a jeweller's shop on Silver Street. When they saw that they had been observed, one called out a warning in a Devonian or Cornish accent. Both ran off, one dropping a carpenter's saw and file. They disappeared up Edge Terrace, which is a cul-de-sac. The police gave chase, but just before rounding the corner two doors were heard slamming, and when they could look down the street, Edge Terrace was deserted. The only houses in the street are in either Edge Terrace or Reservoir Cottages.'

Which two individuals would the children wish to question about this crime? Ask them to list full names, addresses, ages, trades and birthplaces of suspects.

Data-handling programs available

There are many suitable relational data-handling programs for primary school use, but it is probably best, at least initially, to choose one program and to get to know it really well. It would be sensible to check

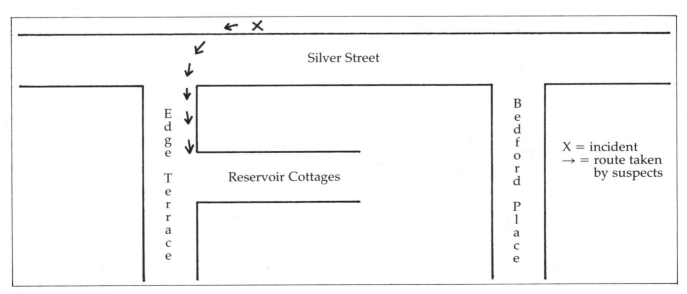

Figure 3

with your local authority microcomputer adviser to discover if a particular program is supported in your area. This will give you access to easily available local advice, and you may be able to share data with other local schools.

There are five programs fairly widely available:

Ourfacts is a simple introductory information handling program suitable for children aged six and above. *Ourfacts* is menu driven. It has very limited capabilities, uses non-standard terms and has a very limited graphics capability. However, it is very simple to operate. It is available on BBC and Nimbus.

Grass is a program with some supporting graphics. It is suitable for children of seven upwards. It is menu driven, and simple to use. It is available on BBC, 480Z and Nimbus.

Dataprobe is a highly graphic program, suitable for children aged eight upwards. *Dataprobe* is command driven and features an easy language with prompts. It has a slow operation, many graphic capabilities including maps. It is available on BBC and RML480Z.

Key is a new sophisticated package, suitable for children aged nine upwards. *Key* is menu/command driven and has fast operation and good graphic capabilities including maps. It is available on BBC and Nimbus.

Quest is a complex program with very sophisticated features, suitable for children over the age of ten. *Quest* is command driven but the command language is quite difficult. It has fast operation, fairly good graphic capabilities and is available on BBC and Nimbus.

Tree-type data handling programs

The relational programs described so far show the connections between pieces of data. One other common type of data-handling program is the tree-type program

Check to see what programs are supported in your area.

which is based on creating classifications about data. This asks a series of questions about an object that the user has thought of, the answer to which can be yes or no. Each answer usually prompts a further question. Eventually the program will offer a suggestion of what the object is: if it is incorrect the user is asked to devise a question that will distinguish the actual object from the guess. This question is then added to the program's repertoire.

This example demonstrates the operation:

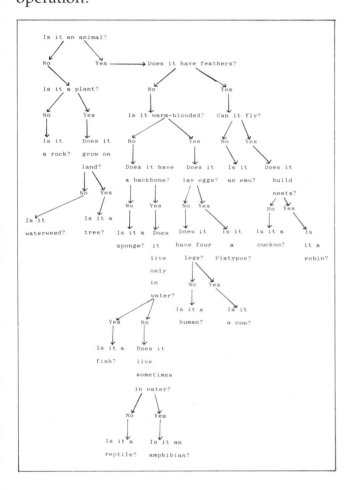

At each point the user is presented with one question, and they select the

appropriate answer, either yes or no. This generates a fresh question, each with a yes/no answer.

Suppose a child had in mind a sheep when tackling this tree arrangement. He would follow the questions describing it as an animal, without feathers, not laying eggs, with four legs. What would happen then?

Computer: Is it a cow?
Child: No.
Computer: What is this object?
Child: A sheep.
Computer: Give a question that distinguishes a sheep from a cow.
Child: Can its hair be turned into fabric?
Next time the program is used, perhaps with a goat in mind, a new question will be added. After replying 'yes' to the question about four legs:
Computer: Can its hair be turned into fabric?
Child: Yes.
Computer: Is it a sheep?
If the answer had been 'no' to the previous question, the computer would have asked, 'Is it a cow?'.

These hierarchical databases (as opposed to the relational databases described above) allow the questioner to build up long strings of questions. It can require quite a degree of logical thought to build up the basis of a satisfactory tree – it is easy to make long single chains of questions, and more difficult to devise branching chains that are economical with the number of questions asked.

Data handling is enormous fun. These programs widen out the curriculum, particularly in the social studies and science areas. Suddenly children become able to test out ideas, and this facility stimulates the formation of ideas. It can be enormous fun: it's always vastly educational.

Using information technology

Using information technology

INTRODUCTION

The words 'information technology' can conjure up all sorts of mystical illusions of electronic wizardry. However, information technology has gained in credibility as part of school curriculum development over the past few years and it is sometimes assumed that the mere utterance of the phrase 'information technology' will produce an instant recipe for success with the computer in education.

Certainly, much progress has been made since those first machines arrived in primary schools and facilities available in schools closely mirror those of the commercial world of publishing and communications.

For this chapter, information technology can be defined as data provided through the means of modern electronic technology such as television, telephone and computers. However, as technology progresses, more and more data can be produced and therefore technological developments are needed to deal with the potential sorting and receiving, creating a spiralling pattern of development. Communication systems are constantly in use in the modern commercial world, transferring data, computer programs and conversations from one office to another in minutes. Huge databases also provide information which can be used by anyone who has sufficient knowledge and computer equipment.

IT in the primary school

The computer is in regular use in the primary school as a cross-curricular teaching aid and many children have a computer in their homes. However, the television is still the most dominant feature in the home today. It constantly depicts the latest economic, social and scientific developments of countries around the world, by using satellites which transfer television pictures from one continent to another. The telephone also uses world-wide satellite connections, and enables us to speak to people around the world as easily as dialling a friend around the corner. Children are directly involved with modern technological developments every day of their lives in their homes: this fact alone must affect the use of such equipment within their schools.

The computer, telephone and television combined form an extremely powerful means of communication which can receive videotext which includes both teletext and viewdata.

Teletext

Many children will already be familiar with the broadcasting services called teletext which can be received in homes without a computer. Teletext is an information service provided by the BBC and ITV whereby coded signals, which represent pages of information either in text or graphics form, are transmitted alongside the normal television programmes. On normal sets the information pages will not be visible as the signals are displayed in code format at the very top of the screen and hidden from view. On specially modified television sets these signals can be converted back to show the originally transmitted pages, which fill the screen. New pages of information can be called up by selecting the correct page number using the specialised numerical keyboard. The pages displayed have a maximum of 24 lines, each containing 40 characters in up to seven colours, making the presentation very eyecatching.

The four teletext services in operation in the United Kingdom are CEEFAX 1 (BBC 1), CEEFAX 2 (BBC 2), ORACLE 1 (ITV) and ORACLE 2 (Channel 4). Each of these consists of a 'magazine' of approximately 100 pages which are transmitted in a repetitive cycle, with each page taking a quarter of a second to transmit. Once a page is displayed on the screen it is then held in the memory of the television set and displayed until the operator calls up a new page. There will always be a short delay between the selection and display of the page because of the continual cycling of the magazine pages.

These pages are continually updated and provide the viewer with the latest in news or sports results. The normal television programmes can be watched as usual, but there is a facility to superimpose teletext on to the normal programme to obtain subtitles or to request news flashes which appear in a box as part of the television picture.

Pages of information can be saved to disk.

Quite young children are capable of using teletext.

There are, however, some disadvantages in using the television-based system. Firstly, teletext is not an interactive service. This means that you can receive information, but cannot send back information or requests via your television set. Secondly, there is no function for

saving screen information for future use and finally the amount and extent of the information available is limited to approximately 400 pages across the four magazines. The subject areas at present represent up-to-date information on sporting results, news, weather, travel news and television programmes. These pages are all made accessible through a general index.

CEEFAX and ORACLE do not provide selections of pages specially designed for schools, but there are many which are useful for educational purposes. Teletext does provide an easy introduction to the world of videotext and might be considered for use in the primary school. If a teletext adaptor is purchased and teamed up with a computer station by the relevant software then the cost of using the service is free. Bearing this in mind, teletext gives a useful introductory experience into the field of information handling for adults and children. If a teletext adaptor is used with a computer, then pages of information can be saved to disk and printed out for classroom use. There are now several companies who sell teletext adaptors suitable for most school computers and details can be found in any relevant monthly magazine or computer newsletter.

This added facility may produce some management problems; the computer adaptor must be plugged into a television aerial socket and this may prove to be difficult to arrange in the classroom.

Viewdata

The second aspect of videotext is the use of a more sophisticated system called viewdata. This is an interactive system and allows you to communicate with host computers which hold enormous databases of information.

The largest service, Prestel, is provided by British Telecom and is only accessible by using the telephone. Educational establishments can access the Prestel database by using a service called Campus 2000. Campus 2000 is organised on three levels: level one is known as Campus; level two as Campus Plus and level three as Campus Premium.

You need the following equipment to make use of the service:

- A modem (the abbreviation for modulator-demodulator) which is a device placed between the computer and the telephone line. It converts the signals from the computer for transmission down a telephone line, from digital signals to analogue signals and vice versa.
- A telephone socket adjacent to the computer station.
- A printer with a screen dump program.

Prestel is the largest database in the United Kingdom, containing over 220,000 pages of information. These pages have the same format as the teletext pages. There are several costs that should be taken into consideration before embarking on the use

Teletext provides a useful introduction to the field of information handling.

of Campus 2000 in a school:
- The cost of the computer station equipment.
- The cost of converting a telephone point to a socket point or even resiting a socket point within a more easily accessible area in the school.
- The annual subscription charge to Campus 2000 and the cost of downloading certain pages of information.
- Local telephone call charges which are more expensive during school hours than in the evening.

Once you have installed the system, it is very easy to use and children have no difficulty in mastering the various options to save on to disk or print out pages of information. Pages can also be downloaded on to disk to build up a carousel of theme pages which can be used for topic or project centred work.

It is a modern approach to information-gathering that is up-to-date and being continually revised.

Prestel educational databases

Although Prestel is an interactive service and a database, it is not a database that can be interrogated and sorted for specific facts about a specific subject. For example, it cannot be used to answer questions of the type: 'What is the weather like in Birmingham today?'.

Children will need to formulate the right question and then select the correct section of the Prestel weather pages in order to find out the answer.

Electronic mail

A third system of communication exists that would enable a child to find the answer to the question 'What is the weather like in Inverness today?'. This system is known as electronic mail and until recently was available to schools through The Times Network System (TTNS). Now Prestel education and TTNS are combined to form

Campus 2000. Electronic mail simply means letters and messages (items of mail) are sent electronically down the telephone lines through a local exchange to a central mainframe computer whereupon they are delivered to an individual's 'mailbox'. Messages are prepared on a word processor and saved to disk by making an ASCII (American Standard Code for Information Interchange) file.

Messages can include the children's own work.

Messages can be any length from a short note to many thousands of words and can include tables of results, poems or any other format of page layout. They will remain in the receiver's mailbox until the individual next contacts the mainframe computer to read the stored letters. This would enable a child in Cornwall to ask a child in Inverness 'What is the weather like today?'.

Costs involved

There are no page charges if a school is a member of Campus. The other advantage is that advertisements and commercial initiatives have no access to the network.

100

Campus (level one) contains several databases as well as the facility to send messages to other members of the network. As both electronic mail (Campus) and viewdata (Campus Plus) involve the use of a telephone, they will incur costs of local telephone calls and also the subscription to the user group. If the children are given free access to explore the systems then enormous bills can be quickly accumulated. However, if you can afford these costs, which can be kept within a reasonable budget if a routine is established, then you will need to assess the value of the information available and its relevance to your school's needs and priorities.

The value of videotext

Electronic mail and viewdata systems must be seen as an enhancement of the other resources that are used by schools, and not as a replacement for books and first hand experiences. The value of using such advanced educational aids is underlined by the fact that this information is up-to-date and cannot easily be obtained from other sources. However, they will never replace the first hand experiences of, for example, touching the animals or smelling the true smells around a farmyard. The advantages of videotext are more apparent after a visit to a farm when electronic mail and Prestel education might provide answers to the many questions that only another visit would satisfy.

One important factor when using this advanced mode of communication is to define a need for using it; if you cannot find that need, then the system should not be used.

Sound educational aims should be defined if children are to use the system successfully; this must extend beyond using the computer for the sake of using something new. Unfortunately, with the rapid progress of computer technology,

Videotext cannot replace the use of books.

teletext can be seen as an easy introduction to the world of information handling as the new pages required are selected by pressing the appropriate three digit number.

Introduction to an index

Working through the index of the magazines gives children an exciting introduction to the use of an index. This can be used to develop the concept of alphabetical order and how to use the index in reference books.

Videotext can help explain the use of indexes.

children are only too eager to explore new electronic wizardry, with the result that all too often the true potential of the equipment and its underlying educational aims are not fulfilled. We must remember that this technology is there as an aid; it should not be used just because it is there, but because it has a purpose.

Management of videotext

There are also some management problems that need to be solved if these videotext systems are to be part and parcel of a working classroom. If teletext is to be incorporated into class work then a television aerial socket must be installed in or adjacent to the room. It definitely improves the use of viewdata if a telephone socket is installed within a classroom. This, however, is not so vital if electronic mail is to be used, as items of mail can be stored on disk and sent in one on-line session. This session does not have to be in the classroom, but could access a telephone line at any convenient point in the school and at any convenient time.

When used with children, these three services provide different educational opportunities. As already stated, the use of

Reading for understanding

Each page of information can be read either in printed out form or directly from the screen. This in itself is a skill to be mastered, and raises the level of comprehension and provides reading material which is topical and from the 'real world'.

Uses of teletext

A team of children could be trained to download certain daily or weekly pages such as weather forecasts or Top 20 records and to print them out for use in the classroom.

These are some of the other possible topics that can be investigated with the help of pages from the teletext magazines:

- television and radio pages;
- joke page compiled by children;
- children's magazine page;
- weather map of UK;
- sports results;
- travel by road, rail, air or sea;
- foreign exchange rates;
- recipe pages.

All these can provide up-to-date information and the printouts can be used, for example, in science for mapping the weather patterns in different areas and making comparisons with local weather. The sports and exchange rate pages can provide valuable data for mathematics investigations as the children can interpret the facts in graphs and pie charts.

Building an electronic magazine

Software packages which offer a simulation of teletext and viewdata make it possible for a carousel of pages to be designed and prepared on the computer by older juniors for the use of others in the school. These programs do not involve television signals or the use of a telephone and depend upon a selection of pages designed by children or staff.

Programs like *Microviewdata*, *Edfax* or *News Bulletin* provide easy structures for primary children to create an information service for daily/weekly school events. These may be results from inter-school matches or announcements of proposed visits and events. Specialised magazines

Results of school sports matches can feature in an electronic magazine.

could be designed to record experiences of visits or collections of poems. The majority of these programs do not have a wraparound text facility so careful planning beforehand on paper is advisable to ensure that each frame saved to disk is attractive and readable. Simple chunky graphics can be produced to accompany the text and a full range of colours can also be used. These in-school teletext programs are very successful, but time-consuming if not thought out in advance.

Working away from the computer

Valuable computer time is wasted if children are allowed to design the pages directly into the computer, as the information needs to be planned in advance using grid sheets and coloured pens. This provides an ideal opportunity for all children to display their own artistic skills and to draw upon their own experiences. It also encourages co-operation within groups as final designs will need to be agreed upon before the children use the computer.

Stories on the screen

These same programs can provide an interesting medium for the creation of a class branching story with groups of top junior children responsible for an individual page which will constitute an instalment of the whole story.

Each frame is created with coloured text and graphics and is then linked to the next instalment page by selecting the appropriate key.

Screen selection

This method of selecting the next screen of information leads the children on to the use of a database such as the general Prestel database on Campus Plus.

Endless hours can be spent exploring Prestel databases and it has been suggested that children should be allowed to roam freely around this enormous database until they find something that interests them. I do not agree with this philosophy and believe that in the initial stages guidelines are invaluable for primary children if the use of Prestel or other on-line databases is to have educational credibility.

This information service can provide relevant facts which can enhance a class project on the weather, for example. An investigation about the weather can be used throughout the primary school as part of a spiral curriculum which gradually increases in depth and width to include skills of observation, investigation, classification, recording and measurement. To compare their own recorded weather information, a wide variety of media can be used to provide accurate details of daily weather and shipping forecasts. Newspapers, radio and television provide this information and the Prestel database provides up to the minute data about UK, European and world weather conditions.

Observing weather in their own environment and gaining information from a secondary source can help children to understand the pattern of seasonal changes and how these affect their lives, the activities of animals and the growth of plants. The information on Prestel about weather consists of forecasts, reports and statistics for the United Kingdom, as well as reports for the rest of the world.

To understand the downloaded information, the children will need to do some preparatory work. This must include guidance about the use of the system and how to retrieve data.

Key page numbers and key words will help them to concentrate their search. If *WEATHER is used as a keyword from any page then the front page of the Weather database will be displayed. From this directory other pages can be selected. Information about temperature, wind direction and rainfall will have been covered in the daily recordings from their own weather station.

The information on Prestel is clear, large and colourful and the children will benefit if they are encouraged to scan the screen for the main facts they require in order to continue their searching procedure.

The use of Prestel will give opportunities to compare the weather

Children can record their own weather information and compare it with that on Prestel.

Assessing the cloud cover.

patterns in many capital cities around the world. It also gives an opportunity to study extremes of weather such as drought, floods and hurricane winds, showing how they do not follow a regular pattern and the social problems they cause.

As most weather pages incur a frame charge, it is an economic strategy to save pages on to a disk.

The daily forecasts can be interpreted by the children into pictorial representations such as graphs and pie charts, and monthly records can be used to

determine the maximum and minimum rainfall and temperature.

To access the weather database on Prestel you can type *WEATHER (return) or *115 (return).

Children should be encouraged to make a record of all useful numbers especially the ones that forecast or record weather data for their own area. For example:
Page 115 Weather index
Page 209121 Warwickshire weather.

To obtain a description of the average monthly weather in the UK a simple route plan through the various frames could be mounted by the computer station. For example, on page *115, key 1 will take you to page 209; on page 209, key 1 will take you to page 20904; on page 20904, key 9 will take you to page 2096; on page 2096, key 3 will take you to page 20962 which is an index containing statistics about the average weather conditions for monthly periods in the United Kingdom.

These routes will need to be planned out in advance so that valuable time is not wasted each session. Other routes could be prepared for European cities or world capitals.

All this statistical information is reliable and accurate and is impossible to find in books or other secondary sources.

Preparation of routes through other pages can enhance topics such as:
  *Travel or *747 or *1130
  *Money or *166
  *Foreign currency or *16695
  *Sport or *117
  *Agriculture or *103
  *Zoos/safari parks or *1344
TOWNS IN THE UK
  *Sunderland or *22063215
  *Gloucester or *22061936
COUNTIES OF THE UK
  *Hampshire or *12916
  *Cambridgeshire or *12932
COUNTRIES OF THE WORLD
  *China or *14664
  *Malta or *146176
  *USA or *14646

All towns and countries have a key word search facility, such as *LONDON, as do most commodities and themes. I have

Looking for the wind direction.

already said that children need to be aware of the reasons for searching the database and initially prescribed routes can help to concentrate their investigations. Searching using key words will only produce frustration for each child as it is easy to get distracted from the main point of the investigation and become hopelessly lost in the mass of data.

Data can be interpreted in graph form.

Electronic mail

Information can be obtained from children in other schools using the mailbox facility within Campus (level one).

There are over 8000 primary schools throughout the UK and many more in New Zealand, Australia and Sweden with whom messages can be exchanged at the cost of an annual subscription to Campus 2000 (level one) and a local telephone call. No international subscription will be levied.

Campus 2000 (level one) has a primary school section which contains several databases from which information can be downloaded to a disk or printer. These databases can be searched using key words, and from the search, the children can then scan for main titles or read the whole document.

The primary menu contains the following items:
- introduction to the database;
- primary weather reports;
- all your own work: viewdata;
- all your own work: poems/snapshots;
- problem corner;
- information source institutions and associations;
- the primary notice-board;
- the commercial and industrial database.

Databases on Campus 2000

The institutions and associations database contains addresses and information about English Heritage, RSPCA and many more national organisations. The commercial and industrial database contains facts about British Rail and a health database.

The weather report database directly involves children in the collection of weather data from their own region. This is then transferred to the main weather database and can be compared with other records provided by other schools throughout the UK. This procedure encourages children to be conscientious in their collection of data and accurate in their recording. The importance of their weather station is valued because of the part it plays in the overall pattern of weather records displayed weekly on the national database. The facts that are recorded are:
- rainfall;
- temperature;
- wind speed;
- wind direction;
- cloud cover;
- comments.

Using appropriate software, these records are entered into the computer at the end of each week. After they are reformatted by the software, they are transmitted down the telephone line to a central mainframe computer. These weekly results are then displayed on the network so that children can investigate the variations between the regions.

Sending and receiving letters

Links between schools

It is also possible to form a direct link between schools. Weather data can be exchanged on a daily basis and this can prove most enlightening for junior children. Totally different weather patterns can emerge if the schools are several hundreds of miles apart. Children in one school might experience snow, ice and freezing daytime temperatures, while at the same time children in another part of the country may be experiencing sunshine and warm weather. If records of both places are displayed, the pattern and differences in weather conditions can easily be represented by pie charts and graphs. Average temperatures and rainfall will show which school had the best or worst weather during a given time. These weather facts can be extended to include a survey of clothing worn and activities undertaken during a given period of time, thus allowing differences in culture and interests to become apparent.

Weather can be represented by pie charts.

Links with other countries

By using electronic mail it is possible to find out the types of food, different hobbies and out-of-school interests children enjoy in different parts of the world. Questionnaires and survey forms can easily be transmitted down the telephone via a modem and can play a vital role in developing an understanding of different patterns of life throughout the world:

- children could describe their school, homes, families, hobbies and interests;
- write to a specific penpal;
- describe their village/town;
- explain about festivals in their area;
- describe places of importance nearby.

A longer term project could involve a class compiling a questionnaire, asking children in their own school to fill it in, then sending the results to their 'electronic' friends, asking them to complete a similar questionnaire. The survey could include:

- favourite pop music;
- favourite food;
- favourite places for holidays;
- weight, height and age of children.

Information about the locality around their school could be exchanged to learn about:

- birds and animals;
- types of trees growing locally;
- transport in the area;
- local historical facts.

A joint newspaper could be set up between two or more schools. News items relating to their schools could be exchanged and published.

Children can compile their own surveys for an electronic magazine.

When using electronic mail, children will try to ensure that all spellings are correct.

Language development

When children are involved in sending letters by electronic mail they immediately become very conscious that they are writing to someone other than their teacher. Although the recipients of the writing are unknown to them, the children are aware that they are writing for a wider audience than usual, so they tend to make a conscientious effort to ensure that all spellings are correct.

Questioning techniques

Questioning techniques are also developed as they become more aware that a closed question such as, 'Do you like television?' will bring back a reply of 'Yes' or 'No', and that the question that should have been asked was 'Which sort of television programmes do you like?'. This type of open question should generate

answers that build up a picture and an understanding of the other children.

Older children quickly develop an ability to spot which questions are sent out by a teacher and which are sent out by other children. 'Where do you live?' and 'What do you do?' are important questions that children need to ask in order to compare their own experiences with the new experiences described by others in different parts of the world.

By using electronic mail they have time to consider their questions carefully and their speaking accent does not affect their understanding of questions or answers.

The growth of viewdata

The use of the viewdata system is growing rapidly and many bulletin boards or electronic magazines have been set up by individuals or schools. This steady growth is reflected in the number of alternative gateways from Campus Premium (level three) to other databases such as ECCTIS (Educational Counselling and Credit Transfer Information Service) and NERIS (National Educational Resources Information Service). These provide teachers with up-to-date information about higher education courses and about teaching resources that are available for specified subjects. These databases can be progressively interrogated as the search is narrowed down to the information required.

With progress being made in videotext, many children already have experiences of searching large national and international databases and primary schools should be exploring these advances in technology for the enhancement of the curriculum. When a child needs information, the point of frustration is quickly reached when searching books for up-to-date facts. The viewdata systems provide this information in a way that is immediately accessible.

We need to educate for the future and ensure that children develop the ability to investigate, draw conclusions and to communicate their thoughts to others. The

Viewdata information is immediately accessible.

computer linked to the telephone lines by a modem or linked to the television channels by a teletext adaptor is an ideal medium to take the education of primary children into the era of world information. Interactive viewdata must be an integral part of the resources required by primary schools to enhance curriculum development.

Logo

Logo

INTRODUCTION

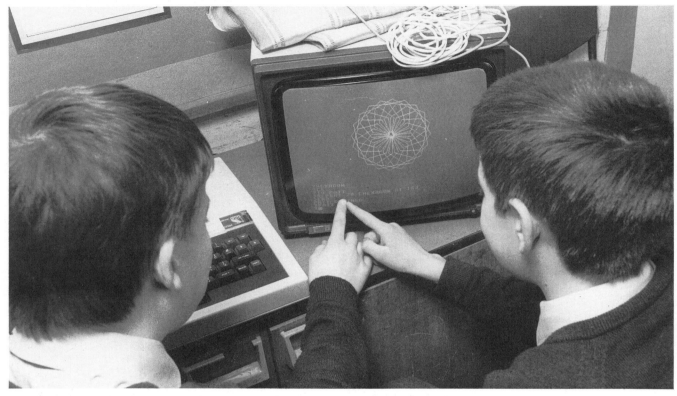

A group of infant children kneel around a toy that looks a bit like a flying saucer. It is round and about 40 cm across. It suddenly moves forward about half a metre, turns and crashes into an arrangement of wooden blocks forming an archway, before making a triumphal two-tone beep.

'That's not far enough. It should have been 60,' one child expostulates. Apparently *Roamer* should have gone through the archway without hitting it.

Sitting at a computer, three lower junior children are deep in discussion as they watch a line draw patterns on the screen. It draws a spiral and proceeds to add a head, feelers and foot to produce a reasonable facsimile of a snail.

A group of middle juniors sits at a table with a large pencilled chart in front of them. 'How about having a secret passage from the cellar to the cave?' suggests one.

'And you need to find a key to open the trap door,' adds another.

A set of chime bars is employed beside another computer as a different group attempts to compose a musical accompaniment for a dog that appears to amble across their screen.

In a top junior class, children are checking some wires that run from a box joined to their computer and to their model lift. One of them types: 'UP UNTIL FLOOR 1' and the lift cage jerkily starts to rise. As it continues past the first floor landing without stopping, another child says, 'I think it's that reed switch.'

All the above scenarios have one thing in common: they all utilise Logo.

Logo is also used to produce electronic noticeboards, write interactive quiz games, draw graphs, solve mathematical problems and investigate probability.

What is Logo?

However well written, all computer programs are limited by their own nature. Logo is not a program but a language by which users can communicate with the machine itself. The user is limited only by the power and capabilities of the machine. If he wants to develop a database of trees that can also draw the shape of the leaf as an aid to identification; create an adventure story that provides its own musical accompaniment or print instructions on the screen for operating a working model connected to the computer, the language of Logo permits it.

Logo is not a subject to be taught, but a cross-curricular tool. Characteristics of learning with Logo are interaction within a group of peers and with the computer, self-criticism and evaluation, and problem-solving whilst developing logic and sequencing skills.

Logo is an application of the computer well matched to the ideals of good primary education.

Why use Logo?

Amongst a school's educational aims are the acquisition and development of skills in the three core subjects of language, mathematics and science in accordance with the National Curriculum. Amongst the resources now available to teachers is the microcomputer.

The time spent in learning programming skills in Logo is no more than for learning operating skills for *Dart* or any other drawing, control or music package. Moreover, once learnt in one application context, the same skills are usable in the others mentioned.

Logo promotes experiential learning, developing real skills in a concrete way through discovery. Learning is less often a case of getting things right than being allowed to make mistakes and learn from them. Logo permits and encourages the experimental approach, promoting logical thought, hypothesis and evaluation through solving problems with the motivations of achievement and creativity.

Using Logo

It is not necessary to be an expert to use Logo with pupils, but it helps if the teacher has some rudimentary knowledge of it first.

There are three main modes of operation when using Logo.

Command mode

When the Logo computer is first switched on, there is usually a friendly message on the screen saying: 'WELCOME TO LOGO'.

115

Beneath this, on an otherwise clear screen, will be the cursor which takes the form of a question mark.

Any commands typed in at this stage will be executed immediately the RETURN (or ENTER) key is pressed.

In the examples below, abbreviated commands are used. The expanded forms of these are also shown. Some systems will respond to either and some to only the abbreviated version. Use capital letters when typing.

Terminate each command by pressing RETURN.

CS   (CLEARSCREEN)

The screen will clear and a triangle or 'turtle' will appear in the centre of the screen.

HT   (HIDETURTLE)

The turtle disappears.

ST   (SHOWTURTLE)

The turtle re-appears.

These commands require no other input. Similar commands you will use later are:

PU   (PENUP)
PD   (PENDOWN)

Many commands, however, require a number input to tell the turtle how far to move.

FD 100   (FORWARD)
RT 90   (RIGHT)
BK 100   (BACK)
LT 90   (LEFT)

Some commands you meet later will require more than one input:

DIV 4   2

This divides 4 by 2. A helpful 'error' message will inform you that the computer has not been told what to do with the answer.

116

Learning mode

Some systems are taught to do something using the following technique:

TO CORNER
FD 100
RT 90
FD 100
END

Once the title line, TO CORNER, has been entered, the question mark cursor changes to a chevron. This indicates the computer is now learning the commands rather than executing them immediately. The familar question mark cursor associated with command mode returns when END has been entered.

Other systems use the syntax BUILD "CORNER and require the ESCAPE key to be pressed rather than typing END.

When the computer learns a new word, it can use it like any of the command words it already knows. These new words are known as primitives.

Operational mode

In this mode, the computer carries out instructions and, unless instructed otherwise, will ignore any other input. It will carry out the sequence of commands it has been taught in learning mode.

A sequence of commands may be entered in direct mode by separating each command word with a space:

CORNER   CORNER   CORNER

Logo encourages an experimental approach.

Pre-Logo games

Games can be devised to introduce the concept of Logo. The major objective in all these is to develop sequencing and planning skills. Additionally, spatial skills, particularly with reference to measurement and estimation of length and angle, will be to the fore.

Playing turtle

Set out a simple maze of chairs. Blindfold one child and ask another to guide him through the maze using commands such as 'Go forwards two steps', 'Back three', 'Turn left' or 'Right'. Only right angle turns are allowed.

Board games

Ask the children to make mazes by shading in blocks on squared paper (Figure 1). Place a counter on the entrance to the maze and ask the children to devise a route through the maze using the commands F, B, L and R to mean go forward or back one

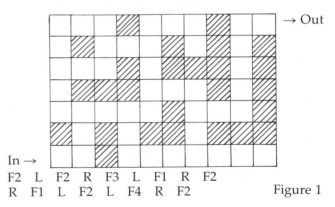

→ Out

In →

F2 L F2 R F3 L F1 R F2
R F1 L F2 L F4 R F2

Figure 1

square or to turn to face left or right. It is important that the left and right commands are relative to the direction the counter is facing. To make this easier, mark the counters as in Figure 2.

Refinements may later be added such as replacing a string of F or B commands with a command and a number so that, for example, FFF becomes F3.

Present challenges such as finding the shortest possible list of instructions to traverse the maze; visiting all the vacant squares; or finding the longest possible route using each square no more than once.

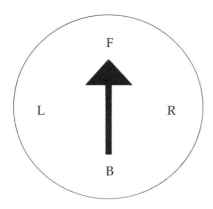

Figure 2

Treasure tokens, made of gold card, may be placed on certain squares and routes devised to find them. Limits may be set to make it more demanding, such as prohibiting more than 20 moves.

Programmable toys

A number of programmable toys became available in the shops a few years ago. These could be programmed by pressing buttons on a keypad. The two main types were *George* and *Big Trak*.

All *George*'s movements were controlled on a time principle. Thus pressing the keys to make it go forward three, would make it drive forward for a count of three. Similarly right three would make it turn to the right whilst its internal counter clocked up three. Although this was acceptable for many activities, it lacked accuracy.

Big Trak was far more accurate, based upon counting the revolutions of the wheels. Forward movements were in units of the tank's length whilst left and right turns were related to the minutes of a clockface; right 15 was a right angle.

Big Trak is no longer being manufactured, but if any of these toys are available to you, they provide an excellent tool for further development of the skills which are necessary for using Logo.

The latest toy of this type has been purpose-built for education. *Roamer* is really a floor turtle that has its own built-in computer and so is independent of the classroom micro. Like a floor turtle, its movement steps are in centimetres (though this can be adjusted) and its turns are measured in degrees. Most of the activities described below for the screen turtle can be achieved with *Roamer*. *Roamer* also has the ability to play notes and control other devices coupled to it.

Free play should be allowed initially with the Logo computer.

Initial Logo experiences

Free play

Free play time should be allowed intitially with the Logo computer. The turtle graphics procedures can be used with either a screen turtle (the little triangle on the screen) or a floor turtle. Floor turtles are invaluable for introducing Logo to young children. The turtle is either connected to the computer with a long length of wire or uses an infra-red transmitter that plugs into the computer, leaving the turtle totally self contained with no leads.

For very young children, a simplified, or one-key, Logo microworld may be provided. A microworld consists of a set of ready-prepared procedures designed to facilitate a particular task. The purpose of one-key Logo is to enable the power of the language to be accessible before the ability to write, or type words on a keyboard, has

been fully developed.

Some computer systems permit the programming of function keys to perform tasks. On the BBC micro, the following procedure will initialise keys F0 to F4 to perform the tasks listed.

```
TO KEYS
*KEY0 CS
*KEY1 FORWARD
*KEY2 BACK
*KEY3 LEFT
*KEY4 RIGHT
END
```

After typing this into the machine, typing KEYS will initialise the commands and a key strip could be provided, where, of course, pictograms could replace printed words.

An alternative is to use this procedure:

```
TO ONE-KEY
MAKE "COMMAND RC
IF :COMMAND = "F [ FD 25 ]
IF :COMMAND = "B [ BK 25 ]
IF :COMMAND = "L [ LT 15 ]
IF :COMMAND = "R [ RT 15 ]
IF :COMMAND = "C [ CS ]
ONE-KEY
END
```

When typing this in, it is important to follow the syntax of the punctuation marks accurately.

Investigating movements

When introducing the language, the children should be allowed to discover as much as they can for themselves. If they are given the command FORWARD first, they can be left to find out the opposite, BACK. Similarly, the size of input can be left for them to discover. They will soon find out that FORWARD 1 has practically no noticeable effect and that a higher number is required.

Investigations can be carried out with a number line. A piece of acetate film may be attached to the monitor screen and the position of the turtle marked. Moving it forward a set amount each time (eg FD 10), the new positions are marked up the screen. Children will soon see the cumulative effect of an action such as FD 100 BK 60. Going back below the starting line (zero) can introduce negative numbers.

The next word to be introduced should be LEFT. (Some teachers prefer RIGHT, but it is harder to spell.) Children will often expect LEFT 100 to move the turtle 100 places to the left and be surprised when it turns it instead. They may be left to discover 90 degrees is required to make a right angle and to discover the opposite of LEFT 90 (which may be RIGHT 90, LEFT – 90 or LEFT 270!)

Free play should then give way to directed play. Challenges set such as, 'Can you draw a box?' (a house, a ship) are the most common.

To enable further development of estimation and planning skills, provide a cardboard box 'garage' and challenge children to direct the turtle into it.

Making shapes

Children should now be shown how to build a procedure, teaching the computer the commands required to produce a particular shape, message or some other desired outcome. A 'storehouse' of shapes can be accumulated to draw squares, oblongs, triangles, diamonds etc. One of the most difficult challenges is how to produce a circle. Help may be provided by comparing commands in TRIANGLE, SQUARE and HEXAGON procedures:

```
REPEAT 3 [ LT 120 FD 100 ]
REPEAT 4 [ LT 90 FD 100 ]
REPEAT 6 [ LT 60 FD 100 ]
```

Drawings may be produced using direct turtle commands and taught procedure names in direct form, eg SQUARE FD 50 TRIANGLE. Many exciting patterns may be created by reproducing a shape a number of times with just a small movement of the turtle between each, eg:

```
SQUARE LT 15 SQUARE LT 15
SQUARE LT 15 (or use REPEAT 24
[SQUARE LT 15 ] ).
```

Variables should not be introduced too soon. Start by using 'global' variables:

```
MAKE "SIZE 100
```

and use a modified SQUARE procedure:

```
TO SQUARE
REPEAT 4 [ LT 90 FD :SIZE ]
END
```

Children may then experiment with the effects produced when they MAKE "SIZE whatever they wish. Once this concept has been understood can local variables or passed parameters be encountered:

```
TO SQUARE :SIZE
REPEAT 4 [ LT 90 FD :SIZE ]
END
```

SQUARE 100, SQUARE 200 etc can now be entered.

Turtle graphics

Just as some commands need no other information (eg CS, HT PD) and some require an input (eg FD, LT), some procedures can be written to work by themselves and others require an input.

It may be helpful to prepare a bank of plain cards about 9 cm × 7 cm on which command words or useful procedures may be written. Notches can be cut into the right hand edge to indicate inputs, while if outputs are required, tabs can be taped to the left hand edge. Cards may then be fitted together to show how the program works

CS   BRICK   LONG   THIN

The card for CS would have no notches or tabs since it is a command that stands by itself. BRICK has two notches since it requires two inputs. LONG and THIN each provide an output so each carry a tab.

Recursion

Recursion is a word that often occurs in Logo texts, meaning a procedure recalling itself. The following procedure shows an example of simple tail recursion.

```
TO PATTERN
SQUARE 100
RT 10
PATTERN
END
```

This will go on forever, or until the ESCAPE key is pressed.
As a variation, try this example:

```
TO PATTERN :SIZE
SQUARE :SIZE
RT 10
PATTERN :SIZE+10
END
```

121

Start by typing PATTERN 10

It may be better to add a limit to this by adding this line directly after the title line:

IF :SIZE › 250 [STOP]

Advanced pupils can be allowed to experiment more for themselves and challenged to draw spirals, perhaps. They might be able to add another input to determine the amount of :GROWTH they want their pattern to assume each time the procedure runs. (Spiral patterns in nature can be observed and compared.)

Communicating with Logo

A different use of Logo for children with a certain degree of competence at keyboard skills is to use the language to aid writing.

An advantage is that only one command word (PRINT) needs to be learnt straight away. PRINT, which can be abbreviated to PR, requires an input provided within square brackets:

PRINT [Hello and Good Morning.]

One other useful command that may need to be introduced almost immediately is TS. Short for TEXTSCREEN, this clears the whole screen for textual usage.

TS PR [Hi there.]

PR [] PR [How are you?]

An empty box following PR provides an empty line.

It will be necessary to move into writing procedures very soon. One suggestion is for children to write about themselves:

TO CHRIS
TS
PR [My name is Chris.]
PR [] PR [I am in class 8.]
PR [] PR [I have two brothers.]
PR [] PR [I live in Cowdray Park.]
PR [] PR [I like swimming.]
PR [] PR [I have a bicycle.]

PR [] PR [I don't have any pets.]
END

A management procedure may be provided:

```
TO GO
TS
PR [Welcome to Class 8.]
PR [] PR [Who would you like to
meet?]
END
```

Adventure programs

Another favourite is to write adventure programs:

```
TO START
TS
PR [ You are standing in the entrance
of a cave.]
PR [ There are two routes you can
take. ]
PR [ Do you wish to go UP or
DOWN ? ]
END
```

Procedures TO UP and TO DOWN will have to be provided.

Successful adventure games require careful planning. Drawing a plan will help (Figure 3). The plan and following procedures, could be written on a series of workcards for middle and top juniors to experiment with, adding to it and adapting it as they wish.

The syntax of punctuation symbols must be copied carefully. Using the plan of 'Ogre Halls', procedures have to be written for each room, titled by their letter. For example, procedure E could say:

```
TO E
PR [You are in the central hall]
PR [of the house.]
PR [There are doors on to the West,]
PR [North and East.]
PR [Which way do you want to go?]
PR [Type D to go West.]
PR [Type B to go North.]
PR [Type F to go East.]
END
```

A procedure, TO GO, would have to be written to give instructions for the game. The last line of the procedure, before END, would consist of the single 'command' E to place the player in the hall to start the game.

To provide greater interest, items may be placed around the house to be found or used. An empty bag must be provided for the treasure to be put in. This can be done by adding the following line to the 'GO' procedure:

```
MAKE "BAG []
```

In procedure I (the study) an option can be provided:

```
PR [Type J to pick up the rope.]
```

Procedure J would put the rope in the bag:

```
TO J
PR [You pick up the rope.]
MAKE "BAG LPUT "ROPE :BAG
PR [Type F to go north.]
END
```

If the children watch closely how this is done, it should be fairly easy for them to add more items to the bag. Typing PR :BAG will show you what you have at any time.

In the bathroom is a window. With the rope, an option may be provided for

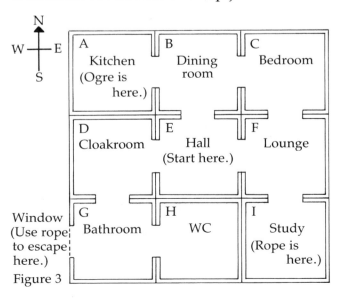

N
W—E
S

A Kitchen (Ogre is here.)	B Dining room	C Bedroom
D Cloakroom	E Hall (Start here.)	F Lounge
G Bathroom	H WC	I Study (Rope is here.)

Window (Use rope to escape here.)

Figure 3

climbing out of the window by placing this line within procedure G:

IF MEMBER? :BOX [ROPE] [PR [Type

K to climb out of the window.]]

Procedure K would tell the player she had escaped.

Electronic notice-board

Using Logo as a communication tool it is quite easy to set up a school magazine with groups of children responsible for regularly updating particular pages.

A simple microworld of the two management procedures, listed below, will make it easier. Careful observation of the listing will reveal how to adapt and extend these procedures as required.

```
TO INDEX
TS PR [GASWORKS ROAD SCHOOL
MAGAZINE]
PR [] PR [WHICH page would you like
to see?]
PR [] PR [1 . . . Forthcoming events.]
PR [] PR [2 . . . Sports news.]
PR [] PR [3 . . . Class 8's outing.]
PR [] PR [4 . . . Jokes page.]
SELECT RC
END
```

```
TO SELECT :PAGE
TS
IF :PAGE = "1 [ DIARY ]
IF :PAGE = "2 [ SPORTS ]
IF :PAGE = "3 [ OUTING ]
IF :PAGE = "4 [ JOKES ]
★ PR [] PR [PRESS ANY KEY ] PR RC
INDEX
END
```

★ This line is quite useful for adding to pages such as JOKES as it stops the computer until a key is pressed (to reveal the punch line, perhaps). Another useful tool is to add a WAIT 120 command between lines of text. (120 will cause about a two second delay.)

Obviously, with the INDEX and SELECT procedures as shown, procedures called DIARY, SPORTS, OUTING and JOKES would need to be written.

Further explorations

Work of this kind can only provide an introduction to the wealth of opportunity for the development of numerous skills. What is achievable with a Logo computer need only be limited by the imagination. Some computers are limited by small memory space or slow processing speed but newer machines have done much to remove these obstacles. More recent versions of Logo boast many more features with great educational potential.

3-D Logo

Adding extra commands to turn the screen turtle into an 'aeroplane' that can appear to move further into the screen or out towards the operator, enables the rules and elements of perspective to be explored. Realism in design can be achieved as two-dimensional plans and elevations are turned to provide three-dimensional pictures. This has much to offer the mathematics, art and design technology areas of the curriculum.

Sprites

Shapes can be created and set moving across the screen with pre-programmed rules given to the computer in the event of collision or over-stepping set boundaries. Much imaginative creative work has been achieved by children using these moving shapes to act out their story creations.

Music

Unfortunately, because of the peculiarities in the way that different computers work, there is no common syntax for producing musical notes with Logo. A look at your Logo handbook, however, should reveal the commands required. It is usually SOUND followed by a series of numbers that may or may not need to be enclosed within square brackets. Two of these numbers are likely to represent the pitch value of the note and its duration.

Children can firstly experiment with the effects of changing the numeric values for pitch and duration. It can be useful to place a glockenspiel alongside, on whose bars the children can write the pitch values of the notes as they are discovered.

Logo is a useful tool for musical composition. Many tunes can be built up from a set of key phrases which can be written as different procedures to be repeated or re-ordered.

The floor turtle is a good introduction to Logo.

Control

Logo also provides an easily manageable language for control work. The following challenge was to ask the computer to do a simple task using standard English.

"LIGHT THE LAMP FOR FIVE SECONDS THEN EXTINGUISH IT" was what was eventually typed into the computer. Each word was the Logo procedure shown:

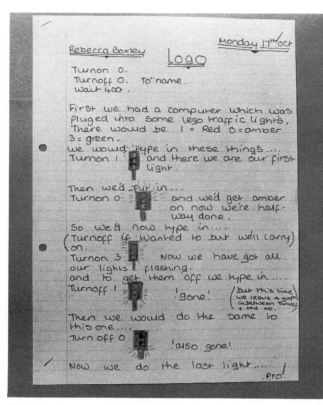

Written work on Logo control technology.

```
TO LIGHT :DEVICE       TO THE :OBJECT
TURNON :DEVICE             OP :OBJECT
END                              END


TO LAMP       TO FOR :NUMBER :UNITS
OP 1              WAIT :NUMBER * :UNITS
END                              END


TO FIVE                     TO SECONDS
OP 5                            OP 60
END                              END


TO THEN    TO EXTINGUISH :DEVICE
END                  TURNOFF :DEVICE
                                 END

TO IT

OP THE LAMP
END
```

The function of the word THE to link the object to the verb was noted. THEN was discovered to play no part other than to keep events in sequence. Acceptable one word synonyms had to be found for TURNON and TURNOFF. The function of the pronoun, IT, was quite obvious.

We can store any procedure into ... sounds ...

TO HEXAGON.

REPEAT 6 [FD 150 RT 60

END

[23:4

Managing Logo learning

The key point to remember is that the teacher's role is as facilitator rather than as fount of all knowledge.

Children must be allowed to discover things for themselves and be allowed to make mistakes. There are times for intervention by the teacher, particularly when children are learning a new technique. However, the teacher should never be afraid to admit he does not know all the answers and should be prepared to answer questions such as 'How can I . . . ?' with 'I'm not sure. Have you tried . . . ? Let me know if it works.' In this way the teacher can be seen to be learning alongside the children.

Discussion is inevitable, and indeed is to be encouraged, so it is inadvisable to have a Logo group sited next to a group trying to read quietly.

Much work can, and will, be done away from the keyboard but there are times when prolonged computer access will be required. With one Logo computer in a class and several groups wishing to use it, careful consideration has to be given to timetabling.

Children can be made aware of these problems and to an extent can be managers of their own time. A timetable can be placed near the computer showing when it is available for Logo groups. A sense of fairness and consideration of others may be achieved as children negotiate for 'a little longer to finish typing in these procedures' or say 'we won't need it then as we'll be working out what to write'.

Ideally, there would be enough computers for each group to have access to one at any time. Perhaps with the falling costs of technology, this may become a possibility in the future, but there will be times when children become frustrated by having to wait. Awareness and sensitivity are required by the teacher to foresee when these situations will occur and to have alternative activities readily accessible to the pupils.

Control technology

Control technology

INTRODUCTION

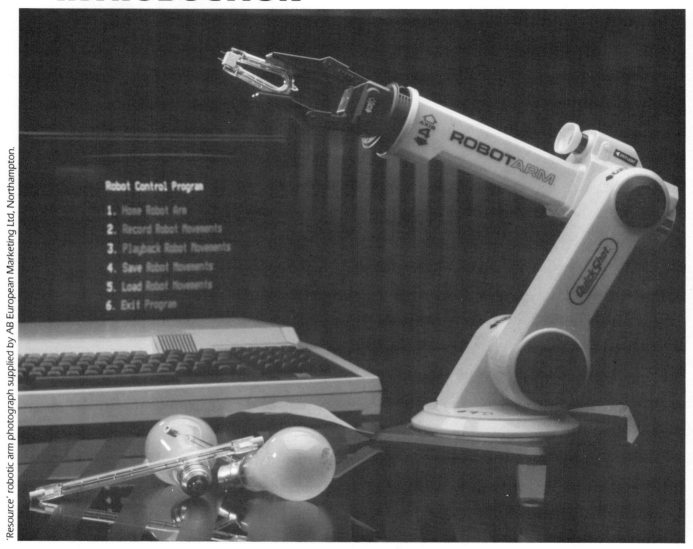

'Resource' robotic arm photograph supplied by AB European Marketing Ltd, Northampton.

The robotic arm shown here is a typical example of a fairly simple application of control technology. It's a specially constructed tool linked to a microcomputer system. The control devices that are described in this chapter are simpler and allow much more variety of use in the primary classroom.

The technological parts of the arm comprise of a number of joints, each moved by a pair of simple electric motors. The control element consists of a short computer program that will set the motors on and off at either predetermined times or when certain conditions are met, so that the arm will perform a particular sequence of movements. Although this arm has several joints, there are essentially four sets of motors, generally arranged as opposing pairs. One set of motors can move the arm from left to right; one set can move the arm up and down; and a third set move the arm backwards and forwards. Controlling the amount of time that each motor is switched on will exactly determine the final position of the grab at the end of the arm. The fourth pair of motors can open and close the grab: these too can be controlled by the length of time that power is supplied to the motor. The grab also has within it a pressure sensitive switch that can control the motor closing the grab. By adjusting the sensitivity of this switch, the grab can close around a delicate object such as an egg without breaking the shell.

The sequence to control moving a pile of wooden bricks from one point to another illustrates the kind of analysis and synthesis that can be developed through the use of control technology. The position of the grab must be moved from the starting point to above the top brick on the pile; the grab must open, descend and then close around the uppermost brick. Then it must raise the brick slightly (so as not to knock over the bricks underneath), and then the whole arm move to the position in which the new

pile is to be built – but as this will be the bottom brick, the arm will need to be at a lower level. The grab opens and the brick is deposited. The arm must now return to the original pile, but at a level one brick lower than before. When it returns to the new pile, it must position the second brick one brick higher than before (Figure 1).

Those of you familiar with Logo will recognise that a simple pattern or loop of instructions is developing in this sequence, with a variable in the expression that determines the height. Once a sequence is written (and it is surprising how simple this can be), the whole operation can be repeated automatically, again and again. With a little ingenuity, the sequence can work with a variable number of bricks in the pile, or various size bricks. Adding a sensor element to the arm would allow the computer to work out how many bricks there were in the pile, and to make the appropriate actions.

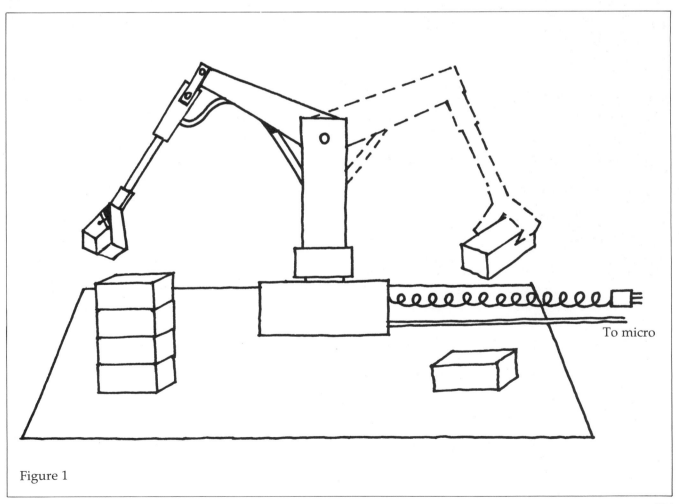

Figure 1

Why use control technology?

How can these principles be used in primary education? There are three sound educational reasons for introducing simple control technology in primary schools.

Computer appreciation

Firstly, control technology further develops children's appreciation of the influence, power and limitations of the use of computers. Control technology applications are now widespread in industry. It's easy to see why: the arm described above could hold a paint spray and accurately paint objects passing by on a conveyor belt. It will do so in a way that uses the most economical amount of paint, and work accurately, efficiently and uncomplainingly for 24 hours a day, if necessary. Children soon understand both the industrial and social implications of the potential changes that control technology is bringing about. They are capable of discussing the disadvantages that automation might bring,

particularly in areas of the country where parents are affected by high unemployment rates. They may also see the ending of monotonous and repetitive tasks as an advance.

Developing CDT

Secondly, and more specifically, using control technology in primary schools can provide an important fillip to work in craft, design and technology. CDT has generally been an undervalued area of the primary curriculum.

One reason for this may well be that children's models often do not 'work' very well. They may be good representations, but the providing of motive power so that they behave realistically is often beyond the reach of children. Control technology can provide the means to make models work in an authentic fashion – so that, for example, buggies can be made to move and be steered from a distance, or even negotiate their own way around an obstacle, or traffic

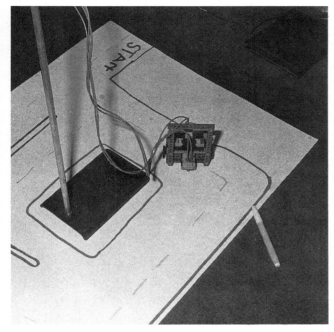

Buggies can be steered from a distance.

lights can perform automatically in sequence.

This added dimension to designing and building provides a very real incentive to make more accurate models, either using traditional craft materials or using constructional kits such as Lego or Fischer Technic. Many of these kits now come with their own control technology packages, though these are not necessary as more general control technology packages can control models from kits equally well. There have been interesting developments of simple wood and card systems for construction, so that children can easily build models sufficiently accurate to work – and to be controlled.

The following construction system has been developed by David Jinks. He recommends a simple tool kit:
- junior hacksaw,
- scissors,
- rule (preferably metal),
- pencil,
- brush,
- bench-hook,
- craft knife,
- hand-drill with 4.5 mm bit,
- paper punch,
and the following construction materials:
- card,
- PVA adhesive,
- wood (10 mm×10 mm),
- lolly sticks,
- dowel rod (4.5 mm diameter),
- masking tape.

The essential technique is cutting the wooden strips squarely, using the bench-hook and hacksaw, and holding joints firmly together at right angles using triangles of card stuck with PVA adhesive. Simple buggies and more elaborate structures can be quickly made, all of surprising strength (Figure 2).

Wheels can be made from circles of card, with lolly stick strengthening. Masking tape gives a solid perimeter to the wheel. Paper punch holes allow dowel axles to be inserted into card, or holes can be drilled into the wooden frames.

Further details can be found in *Design and Technology 5–12* by Pat Williams and David Jinks (The Falmer Press).

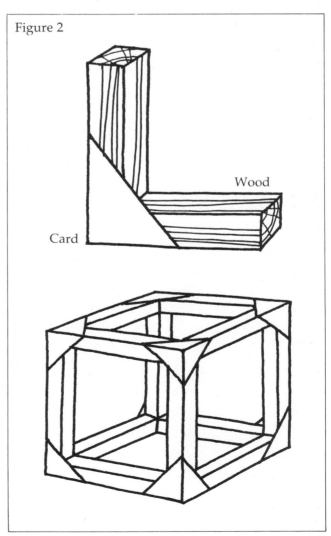

Figure 2

Wood

Card

Analysis and synthesis

The third, and perhaps most important contribution that control technology can make to children's education is in the area of cognitive development. The intellectual processes that are involved in trying first to analyse the desired sequence of events, and secondly to synthesise these into a series of linked instructions, are important skills. The motivation of control technology provides very powerful encouragement. As with Logo, word processing and information handling, the ability of the computer to save successful moves and to obliterate failures without trace is a great incentive to the young learner, positively encouraging experimentation.

The analysis of how one wants a designed object to behave involves carefully breaking down the movements or changes necessary to achieve the overall desired effect; deciding how and under what conditions each part will move or work; and then constructing the sequence of actions that will follow.

It will involve the development of skills of logic. What conditions are *necessary* for an action to follow, and what conditions are *sufficient* for action? These intellectual skills can be difficult to develop in an abstract way, when children are asked to theorise about what might happen. Where more than simple activities are concerned, it does not always help to build working models from such theorising and planning, because of the amount of frustration and disappointment if the model 'fails'.

The great benefit that control technology brings is that it allows children to develop prototypes and patterns for control stage by stage, so that intellectual and practical skills advance together, each mutually reinforcing the other. Successes are retained and built upon; failures are small scale, can be discarded, and do not destroy what has already been achieved. Control technology thus provides children with a supportive learning environment.

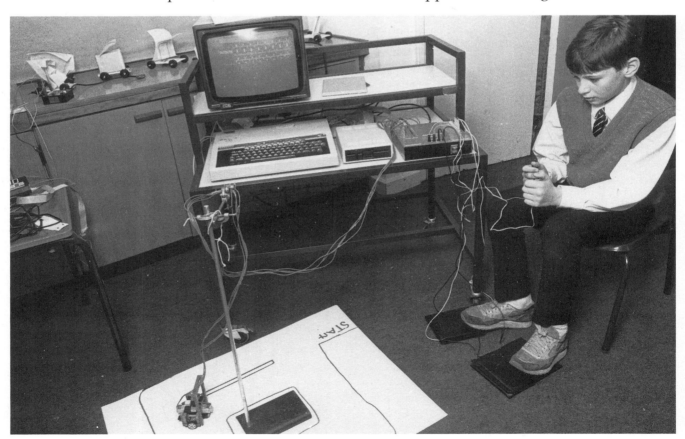

The motivation of control technology provides very powerful encouragement.

134

How it works

Some simple explanation of how control technology works may help. All computers have ways of receiving information, and ways of transmitting information. The most obvious device for inputing data is the keyboard (but there is also the mouse, the concept keyboard and the touch-sensitive screen). Output devices include the monitor screen and the printer. Disk drives and cassette systems offer particular ways of inputting and outputting stored information.

The heart of the control technology system is an input/output box, which simply offers another way of putting messages into and receiving messages from a micro.

Sending signals

The following rather technical description may help you understand how control technology is linked to the micro.

Control technology uses this general facility to input and output a variety of different kinds of signal through the input and output ports at the back of the micro. The BBC micro has two ports, the RML machines a single input/output port. These ports are connected to an input/output box, which allows you to connect up to eight sensory devices (inputs) and up to eight output devices.

Input devices are switches of all kinds – those operated by pressure, by tilting, by strong light, or by excessive moisture, for example. Output devices include lights, buzzers, motors and pumps. For each potential device, there is usually a jack socket and a small adjacent light. The input/output box 'reads' the eight potential input sockets – which are either on or off – and encodes them into an eight bit message. This is sent to the computer whenever a request is made to update the state of the input devices. The box also accepts a near continuous stream of output signals from the micro, which control each output channel, either on or off.

In each case, very quick pulses of low voltage electric current are sent into or out of the computer. In most school micros ('8 bit machines'), they are transmitted in groups of eight pulses (a byte) of either 'on' signals or 'off' signals. Together, the eight bits in a byte can represent any one of 256 different possible messages. The messages are based on the binary code – there are 256 combinations into which eight on/off switches can be arranged. Input and output devices respectively decode and encode each byte, and pass them on to the micro, or interpret them to the screen or printer as individual characters.

Other functions

Because the electrical impulses to and from the micro are so slight, the input/output box has two other important functions. The power from the micro in the messages is too low to power light bulbs or electric motors, for example. Each output has a relay associated with it that can switch on a larger current (often 6 v or 12 v), often from a transformer in the input/output box, sufficient to power a small motor or some light bulbs, for example.

Similarly, because input devices use much larger quantities of electricity than the micro (albeit only 4.5 v from a battery, or 6 – 12 v with a transformer) the input/output box contains safety buffers to prevent the full power supply surging directly into the micro (and thus destroying the micro!).

The input/output box is operated by a control technology program in the computer. This allows the user to select particular output channels, switching them on or off, and to read the state of the eight input channels.

Immediate and procedural modes

These functions can be done in one of two ways. In the *immediate command mode*, the instructions you type in are carried out at once. In *procedural mode* you can compose a simple sequence of instructions that will all be carried out, in order, when you give a single overall command. This is rather similar to the two modes in which Logo graphics can be used (see Chapter Seven). An example will begin to make these processes clear.

Connect a light bulb to output channel 1 by plugging it in to socket 1 (Figure 3). Enter the command at the keyboard 'Switch on 1': the bulb will light up. Type in 'Switch

136

off 1': the bulb will go out. You are now, in immediate command mode, using a computer worth several hundred pounds as a light switch!

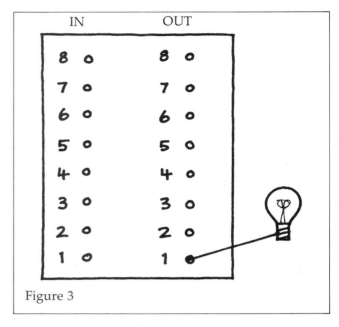

Figure 3

Now try writing a set of instructions in *procedural mode*. Type 'MAKE FLASH'. The term 'make' switches the program to procedural mode, and 'flash' is identified as the name of a new procedure that is to be defined. When you now type in the first line of your procedure, 'Switch on 1', the light does *not* come on. Type the second line, 'Switch off 1', and finish with a third line, 'end'. The program now automatically returns to immediate mode: type 'FLASH' and the procedure you created will run. You will, however, have to watch very closely to see anything, because the light will switch off again immediately after it has switched on, as the computer follows each line of the procedure in turn:

Procedure: FLASH

Switch on 1
Switch off 1
End

To let the light stay on for a while, you will need to insert an extra instruction between the 'on' and the 'off'. Typing 'EDIT FLASH' will revert the program to procedural mode and allow you to add, modify and delete lines. Adding 'Wait 1000' will give a pause of 1000 millisecond (one second) before the next line is carried out:

Procedure: FLASH

Switch on 1
Wait 1000
Switch off 1
End

The procedure can be made to repeat itself in one of two ways. Adding an initial line of 'Repeat 30' will cause the procedure to repeat 30 times; adding a line 'flash' before 'end' will give the effect of recursion

(though this is only available in some control technology programs). However, in both cases a line 'Wait 1000' must also be added *after* 'Switch off 1', or the pause between switching off and on again will be too short to see.

Procedure: FLASH

(With Repeat)	(With Recursion)
Repeat 30	Switch on 1
Switch on 1	Wait 1000
Wait 1000	Switch off 1
Switch off 1	Wait 1000
Wait 1000	FLASH
End	End

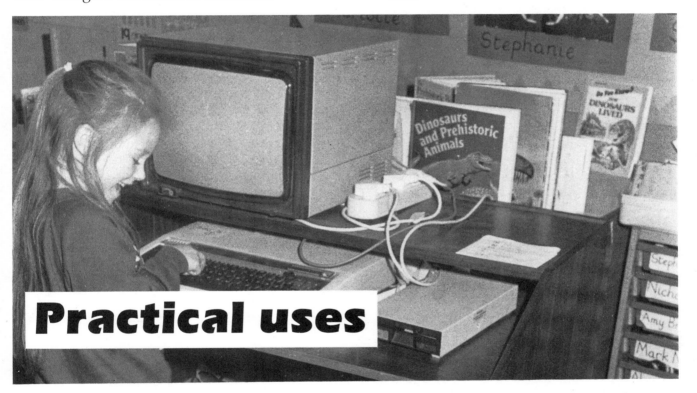

Practical uses

Traffic lights

As an introductory exercise in control technology, try creating a set of traffic lights. This will probably involve you in some initial observations to note the precise sequence that the lights come on, and the lengths of time involved (though you would be advised to scale down the actual times in your model). Use output channels 1 to 3, each connected to a light bulb. Channel 3 could be red, channel 2 amber, and channel 1 green. Your eventual

procedure might look rather like this:

Procedure: TRAFFIC

Switch on 3	red
Wait 5000	
Switch on 2	red + amber
Wait 1000	
Switch off 2 and 3	
Switch on 1	green
Wait 5000	
Switch off 1	
Switch on 2	amber

Wait 1000
Switch off 2
TRAFFIC   back to start
End

Then add the set of lights controlling the road. Use channels 4 to 6 for these lights, and work out how they will operate in conjunction with the first set. This sets up a more complex pattern of lights.

Procedure: TRAFFIC2

Switch on 3 and 4   red   green
Wait 5000
Switch off 4
Switch on 2 and 5   red/amber   amber
Wait 1000
Switch off 2, 3 and 5
Switch on 1 and 6   green   red
Wait 5000
Switch off 1
Switch on 2 and 5   amber   red/amber
Wait 1000
Switch off 2, 5 and 6
TRAFFIC2   back to start
End

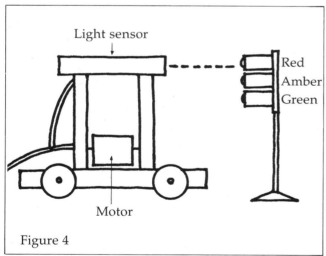

Light sensor

Red
Amber
Green

Motor

Figure 4

This is now using six output channels: what could the remaining two channels be used for? One idea might be to make a buggy (which, as will be explained, will need two output channels to control the motor), and to use an input channel attached to a light-sensitive switch fixed to the buggy. Set at the right height, and with the sensitivity to react to the red lights (numbers 3 and 6), the buggy could be made to stop whenever

138

it came up to a red light (Figure 4):

if input 1 is on
then switch off 7

A second light sensitive switch set at the green light level (numbers 1 and 4) could start the buggy in motion again:

if input 2 is off
then switch on 7

Input devices

There is a variety of input devices available: many of them are inexpensive to buy, or can be safely made with homemade materials. Remember that the objective is to form some kind of switch, or the completion of an electrical circuit. A tilt switch, for example, can consist of two pieces of wire set in a small sealed glass bulb with a globule of mercury. When the bulb is tilted one way, the mercury bridges the two wires; tilted the other way the circuit is broken.

A home made device might be a marble covered in aluminium foil put into the plastic containers in which 35 mm film is sold. Two wires pushed through the base complete the circuit (Figure 5).

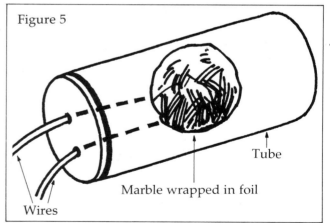

Figure 5

Tube

Marble wrapped in foil

Wires

Pressure sensitive switches are popular with children, and can be made with foil strips separated with polystyrene granules.

Light sensitive switches may need adjusting to the correct sensitivity. Small cardboard tubes can be used to make the light source and/or the sensor directional.

Clipping the tube to the right length will adjust the sensitivity of the device, so that it is not activated by the ambient light in the room.

Other sensors include heat and moisture detectors, and various kinds of touch operated switches.

Burglar alarms

Using these sorts of sensors, children can construct burglar alarms to protect valuable items – or perhaps protect them and allow them to be displayed in a museum. Problems such as this give an opportunity to try out a variety of sensors, as well as craft and design skills. Perhaps two or three sensors could be used in conjunction to deter a would-be thief. Output devices might include flashing lights or buzzers.

This could involve two linked procedures – one to run the monitoring system, and another to activate the alarms, triggered into use only when the inputs detect an intruder. Remember that constantly monitoring inputs may involve using repeat loops or recursion – normally inputs are only read once as the computer works its way past that line in the procedure. Some control programs, however, include primitives such as 'until', which will effectively stop the program until the condition following 'until' is met. The condition is almost always some sensory input.

In the following example, input 1 is a light sensor picking up light from the bulb activated by output 1. If the beam is broken by an intruder, then input channel 1 will register as off. Input 2 is a tilt detector, positioned on the case of the valuable cup. If the case is tilted as it is lifted, then a connection will be made and input channel 2 will register as on. Should both these fail, then two wires lead from input 3. One is attached to the bottom of the cup, the other to the base. When the cup is lifted up, the circuit is broken, and input channel 3 will register as off. Output channels 2, 3, 4 and 5 are connected to a buzzer and a lamp in the room, and a second buzzer and lamp in the police station (the headteacher's office?). These outputs are activated by a separate procedure called ALARM (Figure 6).

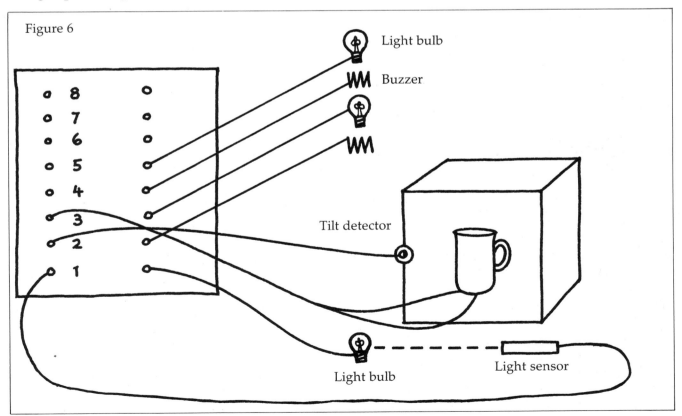

Figure 6

Light bulb

Buzzer

Tilt detector

Light bulb

Light sensor

Procedure: START

switch on 1
WATCH
end

Procedure: WATCH

if input 1 is off ALARM
if input 2 is on ALARM
if input 3 is off ALARM
WATCH
end

Procedure: ALARM

switch on 2 and 4
wait 1000
switch off 2 and 4
switch on 3 and 5
wait 1000
switch off 3 and 5
ALARM
end

When the children have constructed their burglar alarms, appoint yourself as a thief and test the devices. As the children grow in confidence, add to your burglarising repertoire – a pair of wire-cutters and a piece of wire to short-circuit devices will help. Once the children have grasped the principles of these, they'll soon work out ways to outwit you!

Adding motors

Using a motor as an output device is slightly more complicated than working with lights and buzzers. Since the microcomputer and an input/output box can only deal with simple 'on' or 'off' conditions (using binary code), it isn't possible for a single output channel to control a motor fully, which could either be off, working forwards or working backwards. So while one channel switches the motor on or off, a second output channel is usually needed to reverse the direction of the motor. Motors are generally connected to two adjacent output channels as follows:

140

Output 1	Output 2	Effect
on	off	forward
on	on	backward
off	off	off
off	on	off

The type of small motors used in control technology tend to have a high number of revolutions per minute. It is usually necessary to construct a system of gears to slow down the revolutions. This can be done with pulleys and elastic bands, or with gear wheels from mechanical kits such as Lego. The worm gear is a particularly effective way of scaling down movements.

A motor can be added as an output device.

It can be quite a useful exercise for children to use Technical Lego or a similar kit to discover just how much they can scale down a circular motion using gears, and to try to predict the eventual speed of revolutions they will achieve.

Level crossing gates

Another control technology project might be to devise and construct a system for automatically controlling level crossing gates. If a class has access to two computers, and two input/output boxes, it is possible to have one computer controlling a couple of buggies and a train, and the other, quite independently, controlling the level crossing gates.

There's nothing to stop one using two computers linked together – an output channel from one computer's input/output box can connect to an input channel on the adjacent computer's input/output box. Each computer would, of course, require its own unique set of procedures. In theory, it is possible to have a whole bank of linked computers controlling dozens of operations.

It would, perhaps, be more exciting to have two computers working independently. This would give several devices that worked independently, but that could detect the actions of each other and respond accordingly.

Constructing the crossing calls for observation, planning and experimentation. How far the gates can be either lifted or rotated will need careful testing to discover exactly how long the motor must be left switched on. Careful adjustment can produce very accurate results.

The automatic control system will need to register when a train is arriving, and when it has passed. This will probably call for two sensory input devices: light sensitive switches, or some form of contact with a pressure sensitive switch, or even a trailing wire from the train making contact with an aluminium foil plate by the track. The control problem with this task is that while the forward sensor detects the presence of the front of the train, the second sensor need to detect the *absence* of the rear of the train *after* it has passed. Children will discover that they need a way to activate the second switch as the train arrives at that point.

A further point that could be developed is the arrangements of the gates. A gate (or a pair of gates) could swing horizontally through 90° or rise and fall vertically through 90°. This solution might call for four gates, which, with gearing and transmission shafts, could all be operated by one motor – although in practice, a couple of motors would be simpler.

The train and any other vehicles for the road could be controlled by the same computer. This would call for some careful procedures so that the operation of crossing gates was genuinely independent of the operation of the vehicles, but nevertheless controlled by the detection of the vehicles' presence. Alternatively, a second computer could independently control the train and vehicles – allowing them to move at random, but, of course, with procedures to recognise and stop at closed gates! Separate computers would allow children to see that gates and vehicles really did operate independently.

Buggies and vehicles

Quite complex vehicles and buggies can be constructed and controlled with control technology. It is possible to build a turtle and to control it, Logo fashion, for example. Two paired motors are needed for this, so that they can work either in opposition (to produce rotation, turning on the spot) or in unison, to produce movement. Procedure would need to be arranged as shown below and in Figure 7.

Procedure	Motor 1	Motor 2	Outputs 1	2	3	4
Left	Forward	Reverse	On	Off	On	On
Right	Reverse	Forward	On	On	On	Off
Forward	Forward	Forward	On	Off	On	Off
Backward	Reverse	Reverse	On	On	On	On

The degree of rotation that is required, on the distance that the turtle will travel, will be controlled by the length of time that the motors are switched on. Each procedure – left, right, etc, can have a variable attached which indicates the length of time the motors remain on. For example, if one degree of rotation was achieved by a tenth of a second's movement of the motors then a 90° turn right might look rather like this:

Procedure: RIGHT90

Time=100 × 90
Switch on 1, 2 and 3
Wait Time
Switch off 1, 2 and 3

Having constructed a number of primitives, Logo-like procedures can be compiled in this way.

Turtles made in this way can be extended: they could carry a tracing pen, for example, controlled by a third motor through output channels 5 and 6. Or a pressure sensitive switch could be placed in front, so that if a buggy meets an obstruction, it stops. It is possible to make such a buggy automatically find its way around an obstruction: if it finds its path blocked, it stops, reverses, turns to find a parallel path a few inches to one side, and then tries again, and again, until its route is clear.

These ideas give a few of the possibilities for control technology, and how skills can be built up and extended. It is important – for both teachers and children – to start with relatively simple devices, perhaps using output channels only, before progressing to more complex operations. The development of technical, design and logical skills naturally progresses together, and the opportunities for practical problem solving are enormous.

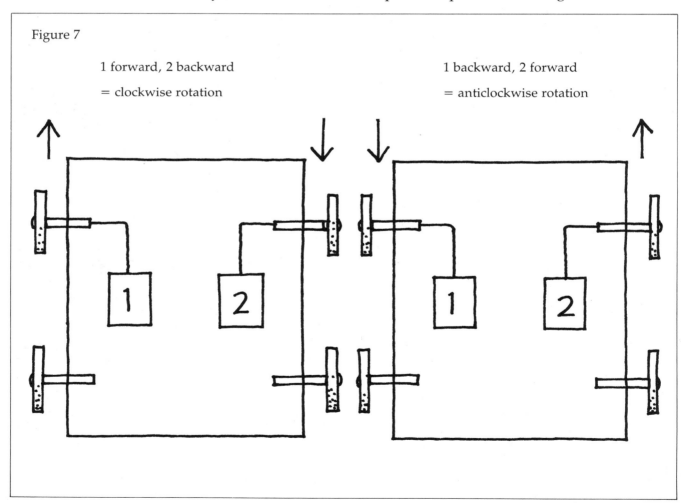

Figure 7

1 forward, 2 backward

= clockwise rotation

1 backward, 2 forward

= anticlockwise rotation

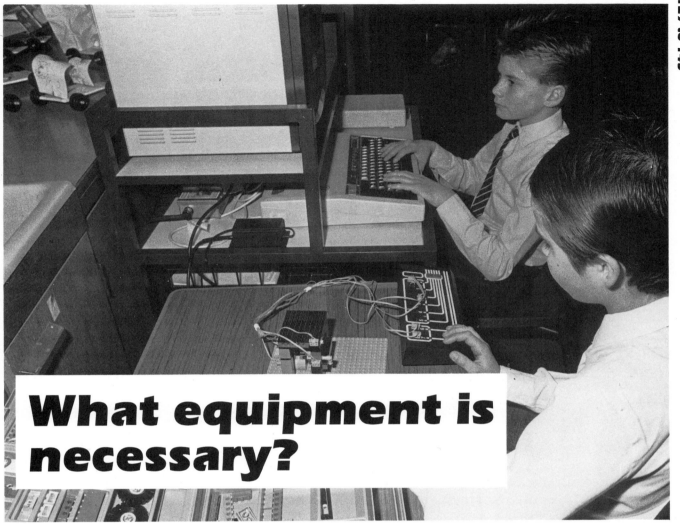

What equipment is necessary?

One drawback to using control technology is that it is expensive. There are three kinds of materials needed: the input/output box, other pieces of hardware and software.

output boxes. These have the advantage that the two functions are quite clearly separated, but it is a more expensive solution.

Control box

Control boxes made by reputable manufacturers will have fail-safe devices that prevent the power operating the devices surging back into the micro and ruining it.

Input/output boxes need not necessarily include a mains transformer to power the devices – it is possible for all of these to be battery driven. However, it is much more convenient, and probably in the long run more economical, to obtain a box that includes a transformer. Some companies supply separate input boxes and

Peripheral hardware

This need not necessarily be expensive. Kits sold with input/output boxes include a wide range of sensors and output devices, usually connected to jacks that easily plug into the sockets on the box. It is possible for children to make their own sensors and to buy less expensive devices. Small electric motors, for example, can be bought for a few pence from some suppliers. Light bulbs and buzzers can be relatively cheap. Switches can be made from wire and aluminium foil. All of these will require jack plugs to be attached, but this is within the

143

These computer-controlled windmills were part of a larger project on the environment.

competence of nine and ten-year-olds (and, because they are only working with low voltage circuits, perfectly safe). There is also the educational advantage that it gives the children practical insight into how switches and devices work.

Software

A control program certainly makes using the hardware easier, and more understandable for young children. Suppliers of input/output boxes also sell control programs that link with their equipment, but programs and boxes are often interchangeable.

It is possible to do without a program, by using a language such as BASIC or turtle Logo. It is not difficult for teachers or older primary children to learn sufficient BASIC programming to write simple control programs. It can be argued that this can provide additional learning points: children learn about the binary code in action, and

also see how control technology is simply another micro application. However, with children aged less than nine or ten, one of the commercial control technology programmes would undoubtedly be more suitable.

Kits are available to build traffic lights.

144

Available systems

Many local authorities have very specific requirements about peripheral devices attached to micros. They may require special modifications to mains equipment, for example. Many authorities also provide specific maintenance and INSET support for particular systems, so it is sensible to select equipment in conjunction with your LEA computer adviser, so that help is available. Cambridge Electronics produce separate input and output boxes for the BBC micro. These, and the peripheral devices they market, are elegantly designed, and include an ingenious double socket arrangement to connect motors via a single jack to a pair of output channels. They also produce a number of analogue input devices, which can be used to produce numerical or graphical displays of temperature levels, rotation speeds, etc on real time basis.

Deltronics produce simple and robust input/output boxes for both the BBC and the RML 480Z. Their boxes with transformers can be adjusted to 6 v or 12 v output. They also market a variety of devices. They are prepared to make a variety of modifications to order.

MESU (MEP) distribute a control technology program through the RESOURCE network. This uses Logo as the basis for the programming language.

Technical Lego produce a wide range of useful mechanical parts, including gears, pulleys, transmission shafts, couplings, etc, that can be used to make the working parts of models. They also produce a simple control system, which being Lego-compatible, is highly convenient and simple to use. However, this is limited and not readily adaptable to other control technology materials.

Control technology provides a very exciting and practical way to develop a whole range of children's skills. Particularly important is the way that practical design and construction skills are inextricably linked to the intellectual challenges of analysis, synthesis and logic. Control technology is firmly rooted in the 'real world' use of computers – both in the sense that it is an everyday practical computer application, and in the sense that it requires children to observe closely and record, to build and construct, as well as work with the micro. It is a rapidly developing and fast-changing area of computer use in primary schools – and one that is immensely stimulating and challenging for children and teachers.

Ideas for further activities

- a mobile crane which can sense objects to be picked up,
- a cat flap, that can be controlled by a single cat,
- automatically opening doors,
- a device to maintain a constant humidity for plants,
- a device that will climb up and down stairs.

Control technology is stimulating and challenging.

Subject-specific software

Subject-specific software

INTRODUCTION

When the microcomputer first appeared in the primary classroom most, if not all, of the available software fell into the category of subject-specific software. This software, which was often written by people who had little experience of the primary classroom, had one specific purpose and the content of the software could often not be altered or amended in any way.

The earliest programs were often tables or spelling testers where the child sat in front of the screen and typed in answers to a question displayed on the screen. Rewards for correct answers were usually a bland tune or a graphical treat.

Fortunately this situation has changed drastically over a very short time and there is now a wealth of software which can be used for specific purposes across the curriculum. Not only has the style of the software advanced, as many packages have been written in close conjunction with teachers, but the level of pupil interaction has also improved. Although such packages are described here as 'subject-specific software', many teachers have their own classification: great little programs (GLPs) or useful little programs (ULPs).

This chapter will take a closer look at this type of software and attempt to provide a structure for teachers to evaluate their existing software so that they can use it more effectively in the primary classroom.

Some of the software described can be termed content-specific because it tests or develops just one particular skill or concept in a particular way. Other subject software is more open ended, allowing teachers to use the program, or tailor its use in a more imaginative way. Both are included here.

Many of the examples quoted are of software that is widely and cheaply available from computer centres, often for only the cost of the disk. They are used to give practical illustrations of types of software but there will often be others using similar techniques, approaches or content.

Most schools now own a bank of software, but it may not always be relevant to the pupils' needs or the requirements of the teacher. This software must be examined critically in order to see how it can be used most profitably within the classroom.

Learning phases

The majority of such software is designed to reflect or improve upon the learning process of the classroom. In planning for the development of a skill or concept, teachers normally identify different phases in the learning process. These can be divided into four parts:

- introduction,
- development,
- reinforcement,
- extension.

Concept or skill introduction

At first sight there might seem to be a wealth of software which is ideal for introducing classroom work. However teachers need to look at programs very carefully to establish whether the software can be used on its own or whether it can be used only after preparation with the pupils.

Mathematical programs, for example, which look at money, should not deny the child the possibility of handling real money, buying and selling from the school shop, counting with coins and dealing with change in a real, practical situation. This cannot be achieved with the computer.

Similarly, work on fractions must

Children should still have access to practical learning situations.

always start from a practical experience and not a screen representation of cakes, apples or fraction boards.

Teacher-pupil interaction cannot take place with a child working in isolation, or with a group of children using software designed to introduce new ideas or concepts. Discussion is a vital part of the teacher's evaluation of the way in which a child has understood a new idea, and effects later development. However, there are some items of software that the teacher can use to focus attention on to a particular aspect.

Patterns can be used to introduce an investigation into triangular numbers. It will give children an immediate and stimulating starting point from which to work. The children will need isometric paper to draw their own triangles as they

'Big Calculator' provides an image of a calculator.

try to generalise the rule. They can return to the computer when they think they have spotted a way of working out the number of triangles in a certain row. The computer will not keep a record of the children's work so these must be kept by the child themselves.

This is a simple example of an investigation which can be initiated from a particular piece of software. From that point it can be used as a part of the work, giving children confidence to try specific examples

150

on their way to a verbal generalisation of the rule.

A program like the *Big Calculator*, which provides a large screen model of the usual four-function calculator found in primary schools, can be very useful when introducing children to particular aspects of calculator use. The keys can be set up to mirror those of any calculator used in school, and a variety of input devices, including mouse, concept keyboards, touch screens, joysticks and rocker switches, enable the software to be used with young or handicapped children.

Used in this way with a group of children, the teacher can introduce the idea of the constant function for repeated subtraction, or how the memory is used. The screen will focus attention and the teacher can highlight particular points to everyone in the group.

Concept or skill development

There is a wide range of software which falls in this category and it is necessary to divide it further in order to understand the ways in which they can be used:
- development through discussion,
- development through practice,
- development through interaction.

Development through discussion

Halving highlights very well the use of software to encourage discussion with the teacher. The program itself consists of a seven minute 'film' of sequences in which a square is halved in many different ways. The first sequences show, in two colours, the square being halved by a single line. Later sequences show different ways of halving the square. At almost all times half of the area of the square is in one colour and half in the other. At any time the sequence can be stopped by the pupil or teacher.

Halving is not intended to be used as the starting point to work on fractions. It should be preceded by practical work on

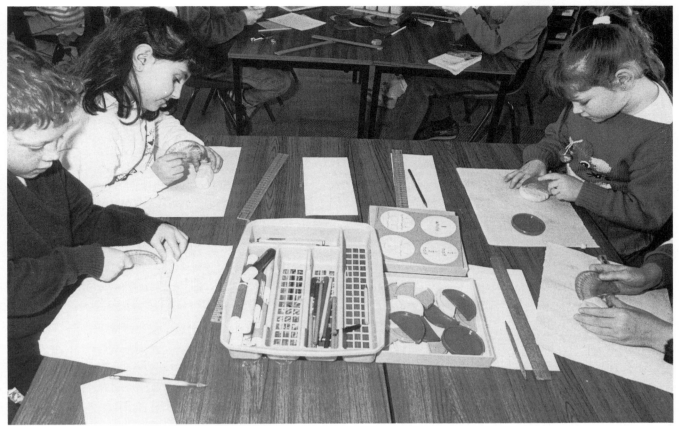

'Halving' should be preceded by practical work on the concept of a half.

the concept of a half, with children bringing objects from home and cutting them in half or filling different-sized containers halfway. Further work could include painting half of a picture, dividing the class into halves, or halving a circle or a square.

However once the preliminary work has been covered and children have begun to understand the concept of a half the program itself can be used with children watching it all of the way through. It can then be shown again, stopping whenever the children wish. The teacher can also prompt the discussion by asking suitable questions:

- What is happening?
- What shapes can you see?
- What does the picture remind you of?
- Is the picture always halved? How could you check?
- Where are there parallel lines?
- What rule is the pattern following?

The children will thus learn various mathematical terms and concepts and the work will naturally lead on to other areas such as symmetry and halving numbers. It could also be followed up with work using a geo-board and elastic bands.

Such initial work should be closely supervised by the teacher, but later groups of children could be allowed to work with the program on their own. Mathematics is not the only subject area where software can be used in this way to build concepts or skills.

Development through practice

This should not be confused with reinforcement software which aims to give a child practice at a particular skill and reports back on the level reached. Software in this category depends on teacher interaction and involvement in the task. The teacher is a vital part of the development process, evaluating the children's responses, explaining results and posing new problems.

Bottles is a program which could be used with older primary pupils. It draws a time/volume graph as a shaped bottle is filled from a constant stream of water. This is a difficult practical activity to arrange and the graphical power of the computer is harnessed very well.

As each shaped bottle appears, children can work out the likely shape of the graph that will be drawn. Once they have drawn their own graph, or perhaps picked out a graph from a set of pre-drawn graphs, they can watch as the computer fills the bottle and draws the graph itself. Once the graph is complete children can compare the two and discuss where the differences have occurred.

The program does not seek to check or score a child's attempts but merely poses a problem which the child can work at as a part of the total concept.

In a completely different area *Micro Map* helps children to develop their map reading and interpretation skills. At first sight it might appear to be purely a reinforcement program but the software has been well planned to provide practice that is carefully monitored by the program itself as it reacts to the child's answers.

The map supplied with the program comprises a wide variety of land types and features. Children can start simply by identifying features at particular map references, or giving the map reference of a unique feature. The references can be given in varying degrees of accuracy depending on the ability and stage of development. Work can also be done on the concept of scale, with children measuring the distance between places on the map and working out the actual distance. Again different degrees of accuracy can be selected and these can be altered depending on the child and stage reached. For the youngest child distances can be accepted to the nearest kilometre, but older children will be required to give more accurate answers.

Development through interaction

This type of software is more self contained, requiring less teacher input. It operates in such a way that development of the skill or concept takes place as a part of the interaction with the user. The software

can often judge the responses and act accordingly.

Perhaps the most famous of such programs is *Podd* which can be used with young children just starting to read, through to middle juniors. The central character of the program can perform 120 different actions. The children can work together to discover these actions by drawing on their existing vocabulary, but at the same time they are encouraged to search for new words. Although children will begin by looking for individual words they soon move on to build sequences of actions. The fact that *Podd* can only do things in relation to itself (uncivil actions like 'Podd can kick' are not acceptable!) and only understands correctly spelt words adds to the developmental aspect of the program.

Developing Tray has been used in schools almost since the introduction of computers. The program presents children with a piece of text from which all the words have been deleted with only the punctuation remaining. The children's task is to rebuild the text. This can be achieved either by 'buying' single letters which are then inserted into the text wherever they fit, or by identifying a whole word in a particular place. Buying single letters detracts from the group's score whilst identifying whole words adds to it.

With initial help, children will usually begin by 'buying' letters. This is an interesting time to watch as children develop their strategies: some will begin with any letter while others select vowels

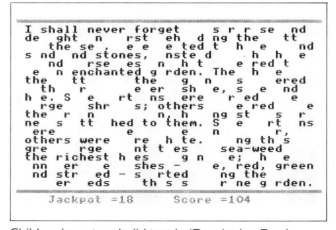

Children have to rebuild text in 'Developing Tray'.

and the most commonly used consonants. Once some letters have been inserted the text begins to take shape.

Children will then begin to spot double letter words and try to fit new letters around them. Short words like 'the' or 'and' are soon identified and the passage begins to take shape. The letter 'h' will often have a 't', 'c' or 'w', before it and this knowledge is put to use in picking out more words.

At this point new skills are introduced with children reading contextual clues. The program helps children to develop reading skills through word recognition, letter patterns, and comprehension. Most importantly, however, it allows children to build upon the reading skills which they

Reading skills can be improved.

already have and to read in a new way, looking for clues from the rest of the text to build sense from the passage.

Whilst the program develops reading skills it also develops group collaboration and discussion. Up to four children can work at the computer at a time. There will be much decision-making, collaboration and discussion. Once the pattern of words begins to develop and children try to identify whole words the group will debate furiously, and the arguments used will show a developing understanding of language and the way it works.

Children will work at all parts of the passage, one child spotting a word towards the end while others work at the start or

middle. Everyone can play a part in the development of the text and all ideas are considered and discussed.

Because the program is content free teachers can enter their own texts which can be taken from books the children are reading, topic work or the school's reading scheme, which will prove particularly useful for children with reading difficulties.

Reinforcing skills and concepts

It is for this area that perhaps the most software has been written, and perhaps most of the worst also exists. However it is important not to dismiss the category completely but to look more carefully in order to use the best of it most effectively in the classroom.

There is again some need to identify different types of reinforcement software and to put it into an educational context. Three main types will be explored here:
- drill and practice,
- interactive drill and practice,
- practice in a meaningful situation.

It will be useful to look at these in more detail and give some examples of the types of software.

Drill and practice

It is likely that every school has at least one purely drill and skill practice program. The once popular *Trains* program was a good

Group collaboration is also developed.

example. Different levels could be selected, a graphical reward was offered for each correct answer and the whole program could be used without any interaction from the teacher. At the end of the session there was no indication of which problems caused difficulty, or the number of attempts at each answer. Tables, number bonds and spelling testers have been the main areas for such software. It is often of very limited value, especially when the user is restricted to the examples within the program. There is more potential when the teacher can add words to a list, or change the values to be tested. Without such facilities much reinforcement software is of a very limited value.

Interactive drill and practice

This kind of reinforcement software usually involves a game of some description where the pupil can use newly acquired knowledge or skills in a more meaningful situation.

Blocks allows children to practice number bonds in a game situation.

Children take it in turns to use the three numbers shown by the computer dice and combine them to make one of the numbers shown on a playing board. The aim of the game is for each player to make a line, in any direction, with four of their blocked out numbers.

Children are allowed to use any of the four rules but can also use brackets and powers to make the numbers they require. Children playing the game soon become involved in a great deal of thought about how to combine their numbers to make a specific number, perhaps needed to win the game. This activity is far more meaningful than merely putting up three numbers and two mathematical processes and asking for the answer.

The activity can of course be carried out with real dice and playing grids but the computer allows the child's responses to be tested and immediate feedback given on the answers.

Nines is another good example. Children work against the computer in placing cross shaped tiles into a grid so that

154

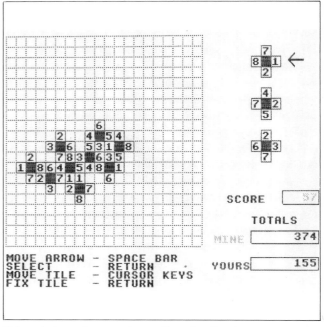

'Nines' gives the user immediate feedback.

they interlock. Tiles have to be matched into the grid so that the resulting number makes a multiple of nine. The player scores that multiple, so 684 would score 76 points. The game is all about addition, using the delightful mathematical fact that the digits of numbers that are multiples of nine always add up to a multiple of nine themselves.

Practice in a meaningful situation

It is often vital for children to practice skills in a situation that is relevant to their own experiences. *Teashop* allows children to practice handling money in a simulation situation.

The children are given the job of running the school teashop for sports day. With a starting capital of one pound they have to decide how many cups of tea to make, the price to charge and the amount to be spent on advertising as well as taking into account the weather forecast for the day. The computer interacts with each child playing the game so that they can input their answers and even change them. When everyone has entered their information the computer decides how successful each child has been and even throws in the occasional unforeseen thunderstorm.

```
Week number    1     Graham
Cost of 1 tea  1p    Cash £1.00

How many teas will you make?  20

How many public announcements
at 5p each will you make?       5

Your charge for one tea?      12p

Do you want to make any changes?
        Type Y or N
```

'Teashop' simulates a business venture.

Children can gamble their money or act more wisely with a smaller profit margin. The program gives children practice in estimation involving addition and subtraction, and multiplication and division with money. There are, of course, other beneficial activities like discussion and decision-making, practical work and costing.

Concept and skill extension

There are many areas where the computer can help children to extend a particular skill or concept. Work that may have begun away from the computer can be enhanced using software which allows children to explore a new area more easily. This is particularly so in the area of mathematical investigations where the computer's graphical or calculating powers can free children from onerous pencil and paper work, or allow them to test a hypothesis easily and simply.

Spirals is a good example. Children can explore the shapes generated by moving in a regular pattern of distances and turning right at the end of each distance. Children may, for example, select three lines of different lengths and then draw them out following the rule that before starting the next line you always turn 90° to the right. When the first three lines have been drawn you begin again from the end of the last

'Bounce' can be extended by observing angles at which balls bounce off a wall.

line. This is repeated either until the pattern meets the start or it becomes obvious that it will never do so. Many different shapes will be produced, some closed and others open.

Children might try to make rules for deciding in which direction the pattern will move across the paper, how you can predict which measurements will give closed shapes, what relationship there is between the number of closed shapes in a single diagram and the lengths of the lines. Once you begin, the investigation can lead in many different directions.

The work will probably begin as an investigation without the computer, the children drawing on graph paper and testing their idea. However, as the patterns become more complex, the speed of the computer can allow children's attention to remain on the pattern whilst checking that their own drawings are correct as well as trying more complex examples to see whether they fit the predicted pattern.

Bounce simulates an imaginary ball being rolled at an angle of 45° from one corner of a rectangular grid (just like a snooker table). The program allows children to investigate the number of

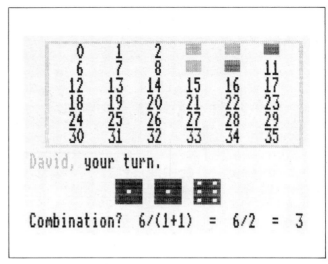

'Blocks' introduces brackets and powers.

bounces made by the ball on tables of different sizes.

Children may begin the activity by experimenting with large balls rolled against playground or hall walls or even watching a game of snooker. The practical work will lead the children to recognise that the angles at which the ball hits and bounces off the wall are roughly the same. Children can then plot the routes of balls on various size grids on squared paper.

Finally the children can use the program to extend their work, easily working out answers for different-sized grids without actually drawing them out, or checking that their attempts to explain or predict the pattern are correct.

The range of such software is vast and within the categories selected here will be software that fits more than one category. *Bounce* will, for example, encourage children to talk about their work either within a working group or a larger teacher oriented discussion.

Blocks may well lead children to explore the use of brackets or powers, while *Teashop* could be the starting point for a simulation project or even a mini-enterprise scheme!

What is clear, however, is that this type of software needs to be integrated into the overall work in the classroom and not selected at random because computer time is available. Teachers need to look carefully at the software to assess whether it will enhance the work of children within the framework of the curriculum.

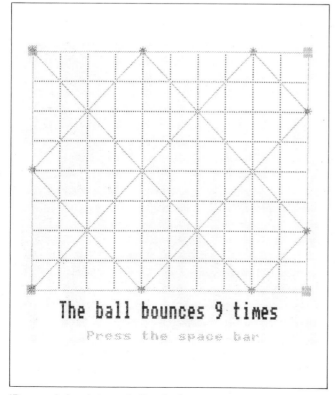

'Bounce' simulates a ball rolled across a rectangle.

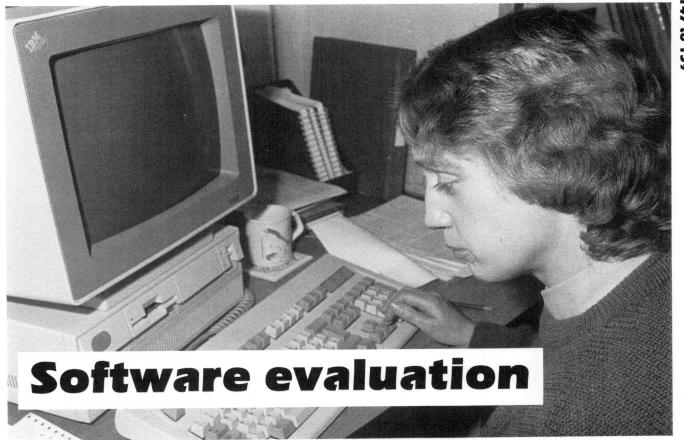

Software evaluation

There are many factors which should affect the choice of software. Many are common to all educational software but it will be useful to identify some of the most important ones within the context of this chapter.

What are my aims?

Clearly this should be the central concern of the teacher. If the software is being used because it fulfils a particular need for a particular child or group of children then it could be valuable. If, however, it is merely used to give children a turn at the computer then it is not really serving any useful purpose. The child's time could be better spent on another activity and the computer used in more useful applications.

Age and ability

Can the content be matched to the child's age and ability? Is the software versatile enough to cover a wide range or is it targeted very precisely to a single user?

If the sub-divisions in a number bond reinforcement program are too large, the resulting questions may either be too easy or too hard for the child. Words within a language program may not reflect those in use within a particular reading scheme or the mix of words may cover too many different teaching points.

Check that the reading level of the instructions within the software is suitable for the child using it. Graphical prompts are sometimes more suitable than words, particularly for the less able child. If there are instructions for the child, are they within her reading ability and can she get back to the instructions page if necessary?

Can the teacher amend the words or questions used by the program or load in their own files of information? The ability to add or replace words greatly enhances a piece of software which can be tailored to meet the needs of a much wider range. At the best there will be a separate program which allows you to create a word list and

157

save it on disk to be used whenever needed. At worst it will mean altering the words within the program.

Are the examples used in the program good ones? If they are chosen randomly, do the same ones keep re-appearing too frequently? Random selections can even throw up combinations that the programmer did not envisage, which can give rise to quite meaningless questions.

Can you select the speed at which questions are asked? If they change too quickly it may not give the user time to respond which might frustrate the child rather than give useful practice.

The visual aspect

Is the screen presentation well planned? This can cover a number of different areas and include not only the sequence of the program but the way in which graphics or words are used on the screen.

Large chunky letters may be difficult for children to read, especially if the screen is very cluttered. On the other hand, small teletext style letters may not be large

The screen presentation should be eye-catching.

enough for young children. Letter shapes may also be different from the style used in school.

Where children are asked to move an object around the screen, the speed of the cursor movement in relation to the use of keys or other devices is important. If it moves too quickly the child will overshoot the targets and become frustrated with the task. If it is too slow, children will become bored. Again, where this is a feature of the program, look for the ability to alter the speed of cursor movement.

Colours should provide a strong contrast where there is text to be read, but should not detract from the importance of the text. Special care needs to be taken when software is to be used with children with visual handicaps. Many of the best software packages allow the teacher to reset colours to provide the best conditions.

Controlling sound and vision

Are the rewards suitable for the child and the classroom situation? Incessant tunes and pretty pictures which are often put in as rewards need to be matched to the user's age and maturity. There is also a need to be able to turn off the sound or even the pictures which can become monotonously boring, and even frustrating after the first few times. However, aural signals can be useful to the teacher who can be alerted to a problem.

Some of the best software gives these options on a 'teacher page' which can be set before the child uses the program. Levels of sound can be turned off altogether, or adjusted to suit the classroom situation. Where a suitable teacher password is used the children can not alter the settings.

Provision of feedback

Does the software provide feedback about the child's responses? Many programs give only a total score at the end of the test.

The teacher should have time for other children.

Whilst this gives a superficial analysis of the child's ability, it gives no direct feedback on the questions that cause problems. The teacher could sit and watch the responses, but this would be impractical in the busy classroom. However, it is easily within the computer's power to store all answers, response times and even analyse them to provide direct feedback to the teacher.

Documentation

This varies greatly from program to program. Standards have improved enormously and much documentation now comes with extra resources or ideas on making the best use of the software.

With older children it may be sensible to ask if they can use the documentation for themselves. In an age where we encourage children to research and solve problems it would be helpful if software came with child-centred documentation as well as a more technical teacher pack.

Assessing advantages

Does it do the task better than conventional methods? This of course is the crucial question. What is the computer offering that cannot be accomplished by more traditional means?

A sequencing exercise could easily be accomplished with pieces of paper which the child can physically move from place to place. A cloze exercise which allows only one specific word as the answer does not encourage group discussion or creativity; a number bond checker could be devised using paper and a calculator!

A program, however, that can create many examples, perhaps for map reading, which would take a long time for the teacher to create, and as long to check, can benefit not only the child but free the teacher to work with other children, or create material in another area.

If there is no advantage in using a particular piece of software, or if the computer is being used merely because it is there, then children are probably better off without it. The expensive hardware can certainly be put to better use. However, good quality software which is carefully matched to the needs of the child can be used to great advantage in the classroom.

Computers for music

Computers for music

INTRODUCTION

Why music?

Music may not immediately spring to mind as the most obvious application of computers, but the two complement each other with great effect. This chapter demonstrates the real and exciting potential of the microcomputer to bring music into the primary classroom. No expertise in music or in computing is necessary; all you need to be is a good primary school teacher.

In the commercial music world computers are becoming as indispensible a part of a composer's or musician's

equipment as a word processor is to a writer or secretary. This move is being reflected in education. The 1988 DES report on micros in schools identified music as a major area of application in primary schools.

It is suprising how much can be achieved without any special hardware or software, and that is what the bulk of this chapter is about. Using the built-in sound commands in BBC BASIC, a variety of interesting sounds can be made using only the briefest of instructions. In fact, some of the one-line programs suggested in this chapter probably represent the best value you are likely to encounter, using the minimum of effort to get the most interesting result out of the computer!

Of course, the best systems need lots of extra equipment in addition to the computer itself, but much of this is suprisingly inexpensive. The ideas which are suggested here can be used by anyone without specialist knowledge of either computers or music. A number of worksheets have been developed and these are used as examples together with some of

the resulting work produced by the children. These worksheets have been used successfully with groups of children working without any help from the teacher. They are given as photocopiable sheets on page 199.

It might help to point out that in talking about 'music', we are using the term in its widest sense to encompass all types of creative play with sounds. Using simple resources and guidelines, various suggestions are given to help exploit a child's natural curiosity and creativity.

Classroom organisation

Music is essentially a social activity and one of the priorities in developing the worksheets has been to encourage group work. Many computer applications involve a single individual relating solely to his computer. The projects suggested in this chapter can, if necessary, be usefully tackled by individual children, although they are much more successful when undertaken by groups or the entire class.

The following equipment is required:
- At least one BBC computer. Two or three would be useful, but some of the

projects can be tackled by a whole class using just one computer. No extra software or hardware is required. The sound quality of the built-in loudspeaker on the BBC computer is adequate for the type of work covered here. Sounds made by the Master computer are significantly louder! Some of the programs listed on the worksheets will produce slightly better results when run on a Master but still work effectively on a standard BBC-B as well.
- Musical instruments such as xylophones,

recorders, cymbals, drums, triangles, woodblocks, glockenspiels and instruments made by the children.

- Standard materials for creative work such as paper, cardboard, crayons, pens, paints, junk materials etc.
- One of the worksheets suggests making costumes and dressing-up, for which old clothes might be useful.

The worksheets

Worksheets were produced so that children would be able to work independently with the minimum of assistance. The intention was to complement topic work already being planned by the teacher. One class was planning work on the subject of 'Light' which gave rise to a set of worksheets on the theme of 'Laser Bugs' (see Figure 1).

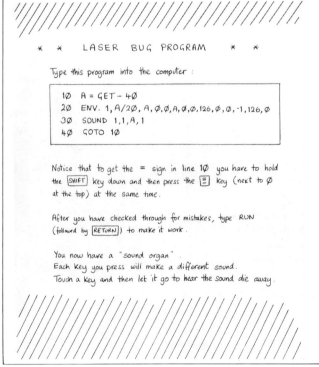

Figure 1

Another class was planning work on the environment. For this class some of the same worksheets were adapted. It was a straightforward task to adapt the ideas to fit a variety of different topics.

No special order for using the worksheets needed to be followed. The

Laser Bug Voices (Figure 2) worksheets were used with one group, and the *Laser Land Sounds* (Figure 3) independently with another.

The traditional view of primary school music.

IDEAS FOR USING THE LASER BUG PROGRAM

1. On the other side of the universe is the planet KEENOIZ where the LASER BUGS live. Laser Bugs love laser light and when they talk they make laser sounds.

   Each key on the computer keyboard is a different Laser Bug's voice. Press some keys and see what their voices sound like.

2. The Laser Bugs are all different. Some are happy. Some are sad. Some are friendly. Some are angry. How would you describe the Laser Bug voices made by these keys?

   Z   4   D   ]

   [P   /   @

   space bar

3. Can you find a key which fits each of these types of Laser Bug voices?

   Questioning   Cunning   Curious
   Chuckling   Giggling   Mocking
   Dull and Boring Excited Spiteful
   Stuttering

Figure 2

Figure 3

There are lots of background noises which the Laser Bugs can hear as they travel around their planet.

You can use the computer to make these noises.

1 CRACKLES

Type in this line. Press RETURN when you have finished.

```
1 SOUND Ø, RND, RND, .1 : G.1
```

To hear the sound type

```
G.1                followed by  RETURN  as before
```

The sound will go on for ever if you let it. To make it stop press the ESCAPE key (top left-hand side) then type G.1 once more to hear it again.

What do you think it sounds like? It is a sort of crackly, crinkly sound. What other words describe it? You can make up a short poem using words which the sounds bring to mind.

The sound is a bit like crackly paper. Try crinkling different sorts of paper and see which sounds most like the computer. If you have shiny paper or kitchen foil you can hold it in the light as you crinkle it. Look at the crinkly light and shadows.

Where might you hear this sound on the Laser Bug planet? It could be crackling fire near a volcanoe, or radio signals from space, or Laser Bugs using the laser phone. Draw a picture of where you think it is.

Figure 4

1. This program makes patterns on the screen. Type it into the computer.

```
1 MO.2
2 V.19, RND, RND(8)-1, Ø, Ø, Ø
3 GC. RND, RND
4 PL. RND, RND(2ØØØ), RND(2ØØØ)
5 IF INKEY(1)>Ø THEN A=GET : G.1
6 G.2
```

Type RUN to start it off.
It will produce a changing set of patterns.

When Laser Bugs go to the movies, or watch TV, this is the sort of thing they expect to see.

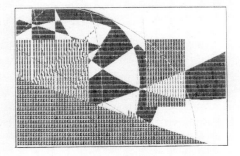

2. RUN the program. When it reaches a pattern you like tap any key to freeze the screen. (The long space bar at the bottom of the keyboard is probably the best key to tap since it is the biggest.)

Draw or paint a copy of the picture you have on the screen.

Figure 5

1. Type this program into the computer :

```
1 ENV. RND,1, RND, Ø, Ø, RND, Ø, Ø, 126, -1, Ø, Ø, 126, Ø
2 SOUND RND, RND, RND, RND
3 G.1
```

Check what you have typed in carefully, then type RUN (followed by RETURN) to start it off.

This is the sound of lots of happy little laser bugs enjoying themselves playing laser land games : sliding, chasing, running and jumping. Can you imagine the scene? Where do you think they are ... at the seaside, or a funfair ...? What sorts of games do the sounds make you think of?

Press ESCAPE to stop the sounds. Type RUN if you want to start them again (followed by RETURN).

2. Some Laser Bugs play funny games which are mixed-up versions of games we play, like leap-frog football, water cricket, piggy-back basket ball and tennis on pogo sticks. Can you think of some other funny games they might be playing?

3. Draw a picture of the scene these computer sounds might represent. It could be a big picture showing lots of laser bugs playing different games, or a close-up of one game. A group of you could make a big picture together. Some do background scenes and others cut out their "close-ups" to stick nearer the bottom of the picture. Before you begin, run the computer program again. Close your eyes and try to imagine what the laser bugs are doing.

The one-line programs in the *Laser Land Sounds* worksheets were typed in and used one at a time with each new worksheet adding to the store of sounds. The idea used in the worksheets, of typing 'G.' followed by a line number to run a sound command, may seem rather unorthodox to some experienced computer users, but it worked well, and proved a simple but very effective device.

The *Laser Land Movies* (Figure 4) and *Laser Land Games* (Figure 5) programs were slightly longer, which meant that it was practical to save them on to disk. The *Laser Land Movies* program did some strange things with colours which at times made the screen text invisible when trying to list it. This problem was overcome by pressing BREAK and typing OLD to recover it – or alternatively starting over again.

One of the reasons that these programs produced such a wide variety of output from a few simple instructions is that they make use of random numbers and random decisions. This meant that each program produced a slightly different result each time it was run.

Children's work

In order to explore new ways in which computer-generated music might be integrated into classroom activities, we undertook two projects.

The environment

We worked with a group of second year juniors at a local primary school. The project was conducted with six girls aged eight to nine who played recorders together in the school's recorder group. The classroom topic was 'The environment'.

Initially, the children typed very simple short programs into the computer to create sounds. These were sometimes only one line in length. Four worksheets had been produced entitled *Crackles*, *Bubbles*, *Raindrops* and *Wind*. Using the worksheets,

the children were easily able to type in the short programs to produce certain sounds such as bubbles, raindrops etc.

The children then listened to the sounds and described them in their own words. Although many of the descriptions were derived from the title of the sound, more abstract connections were made.

They selected one of the four sounds in order to write a poem using images that the sound had conjured up for them. Whilst doing this they made constant aural checks on the sound using the computer, with the idea that the poem would be read with the computer providing the background soundscape.

While describing the sounds, the children had been thinking about how they might make similar sounds using musical instruments. With the poems finished, it was a natural step to incorporate these ideas with the computer to generate the soundscape to accompany the poem. At this stage the problem of how to co-ordinate the sound material and the poem had to be tackled. After discussing various ideas such as conducting with visual cues and using musical notation, the solution of

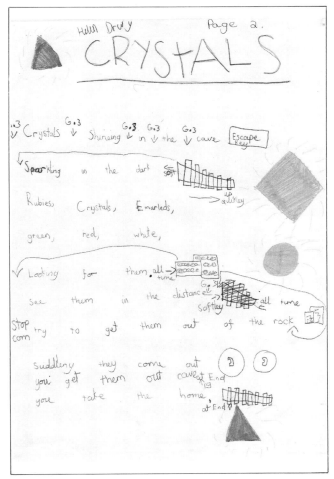

Helen's poem was called, 'Crystals'.

using graphical notation with written instructions was arrived at.

Examples are given of written work produced by some of the children who used the worksheets. Some very interesting notational ideas were devised.

In Helen's poem 'Crystals' pictures of musical instruments and the instructions 'G.3' and 'ESCAPE key' are written into the text to show where the instrumental and computer sounds are to be made while the poem is read out loud.

Having indicated where sounds should begin, the children realised that a way of

showing when to stop it would be useful. Clair hit on the ingenious idea of using red traffic lights as a 'stop' symbol for interpreting her 'Silvery Sound' poem.

After working on the poems, the scope of the project with the computer was extended to more general creative writing focused on an old building near the school. The building is rumoured to be haunted, so the children wrote ghost stories. Again they were encouraged to think how the computer-generated sounds could be used as a soundscape to enrich their work. There was no restriction on the number of different sounds which could be used. More computer sounds were placed at the children's disposal and it was suggested to them that they might want to try and program the computer themselves.

Without any help, Lizzie managed to work out how to modify the single line programs and experimented with ways of making new sounds for her ghost story.

The children tackled the projects with great enthusiasm and were able to survive quite capably without any help from their teacher. As their experience developed they felt confident to experiment and try out new ideas of their own.

Siân's interpretation of a Laser Bug.

Helen's Laser Bug.

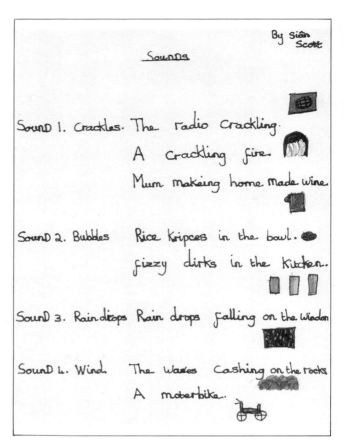

'Sounds' by Siân.

Crackles

C rackles like bonfires
R ed orange and yellow
A fire work going off
C rickely crackley curnch
K athring wheels spinning
L ouley glowing colours
E evening shadows make the fire glow
S udenley it's over

Stacey Leeanne Hurst

Stacey wrote an evocative poem called 'Crackles'.

Light fantastic

An entire class of 30 third year juniors of another local school were involved in a project entitled 'Light Fantastic'. The *Laser Land* worksheets were developed for this group, featuring the *Laser Bug* characters.

Using a simple program, each key on the computer keyboard, when depressed, creates a different sound (Figure 2). By pressing two or three different keys quickly one after another, the children were able to create their own Laser Bug Voices.

The project escalated with the children drawing pictures of their own Laser Bugs and writing character studies. The work culminated in a musical production incorporating drama, dance, use of musical instruments and the computer. All the children enjoyed dressing-up and entering their Laser Land World.

The *Laser Land Movies* worksheets were designed to develop the theme further by adding the extra dimension of computer-generated graphics and visual patterns.

Commercial software

Much of the educational software produced for musical applications is concerned with drill and practice, and could not be considered to have significant potential as a creative tool. Four of the more interesting packages considered here are *Compose*, *Sounds Useful*, *Basic Music Composition* (*The Tobin Music System*) and *Island Logic: The Music System*.

Compose

Compose has been developed by Andy Pierson at the Shell Centre of Nottingham University and is suitable for use with primary school children of all ability levels. It uses a menu of pictures, including a tree, car and house, for example, each of which represents a short musical phrase. Using a few simple key strokes, the user can select pictures from the menu in any combination and in any order to compose a tune. The tune can then be edited until you are

satisfied with the melody. *Compose* can be used in a number of ways; for example, to explore notation and as a stimulus to creative music making, along with other instruments.

The *Compose* manual suggests various ideas for using the program in the classroom. Having worked out an acceptable tune, the program can be used along with the pictures to stimulate creative writing and story tellings. The *Compose* tune pictures can be dumped to the computer printer so that children can write their own words on the print-out. Using available instruments and their own voices, children can copy the phrases in their tunes, or make up simple accompaniments.

Another interesting possibility suggested is to allocate each of the nine picture phrases to a different child, so that one is a tree, another a teapot, and so on. The rest of the children in the group can then make up a tune in the same way as they would have done with the *Compose* program, but using each child to play the phrases in sequence rather than the computer.

Sounds Useful

Sounds Useful is a collection of three inter-related programs – *Synthesiser*, *Ostinato* and *Sequencer*. (An 'ostinato' is a continuously repeated short musical phrase.)

Synthesiser allows the user to create original sounds which can then be used in the rest of the package. *Ostinato* allows a musical phrase to be typed in and then played back with a specified length of rest between repetitions of the phrase. Different phrases prepared in *Ostinato* can be put in an order with *Sequencer*. Instructions have to be typed in from the computer keyboard. It does not have the simplicity of the menu operation and pictures used in *Compose*, but it does feature a rather attractive animated piano keyboard display.

Basic Music Composition

The aim of this program is to prompt and help the user to enter a tune into the computer using traditional five-line stave music notation. It can then be played back with an automatic accompaniment provided. It is easy to use and difficult to make mistakes, though a music specialist may find it easier to use at first than a teacher who has no musical knowledge. The program has the facility to print out a copy of each child's composition in traditional notation with chord symbols added.

Island Logic: The Music System

This is a highly regarded and widely used package, and is one of the most advanced, thorough and well presented application of any type developed for the BBC-B.

Aided by sophisticated graphics, the user presses keys to enter notes in a melody, and can add accompanying parts to build up a piece of music. The piece can be stored, modified, played back with different sounds, and the music printed out if required.

It is most likely to be used for entering scores from sheet music – a very useful package to have available for any children with a special interest.

Music and computing complement each other perfectly.

Adding extra hardware

There is currently only one system suitable for primary schools which is receiving special attention in developing applications. This is the Hybrid Music System produced by Hybrid Technology of Cambridge. Its Music 5000 synthesiser plugs into the BBC Micro and offers hi-fi standard sound quality, much better than anything the internal speaker can manage. The system will do all that the *Island Logic: The Music System* will do, but producing near professional quality sound.

It also has the potential of serving a very practical role in schools where there is no pianist for such things as accompanying hymns in assembly, or providing music for movement classes. Unlike a tape recorder the music can be stopped and restarted in any place. The main tune may be highlighted whilst the accompaniment is muted, the tempo and key changed independently, and so on.

The basic synthesiser, the Music 5000 box, can plug into any hi-fi system. To this can be added the Music 1000 amplifier and speakers, which also permits up to three children to listen on headphones, and the Music 4000 organ-type keyboard.

Final thoughts

Both music and computing are usually thought of as being particularly specialist subjects by nature, so it is possible that a teacher involved with one area may not feel sufficiently confident in the other to link them. This chapter should have demonstrated the reverse; music and computing complement each other so well that a teacher without specialist knowledge in either area can use the rich possibilities of linking them up to develop their confidence in both.

We hope that your appetite has been sufficiently whetted to follow up some of the exciting potential that exists for using computers in music and creative expression in the classroom.

Computers for art and design

Computers for art and design

INTRODUCTION

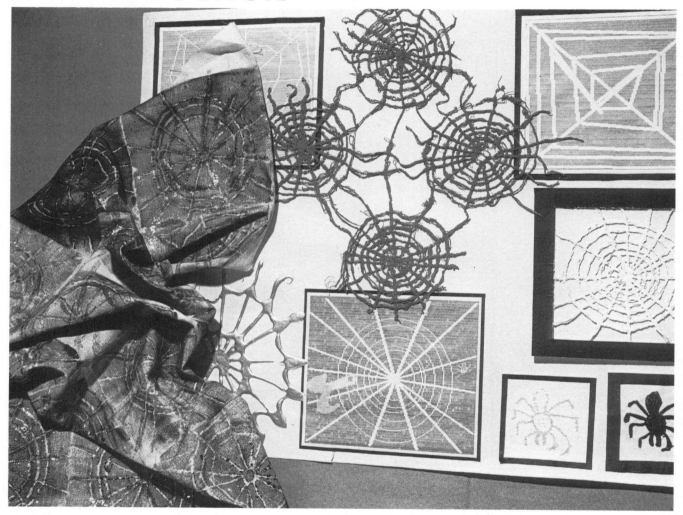

A general discussion about the role of art and design in the primary school might range from consideration of 'What picture to paint on Friday afternoon' to 'Whether it provides the key to our understanding of how the visual sense underlies the whole curriculum'. However, for our present purpose it might be useful to bear in mind three central concerns of art and design as a subject.

The first is the nature of perception: looking, observing and the encouragement of visual and tactile awareness. The second is the use of materials as media, constructional and aesthetic aspects of handling paint, clay, wood, textiles etc. The third is the world of form and the characteristics of visual elements such as those of colour, shape, pattern and texture.

Attending to these three concerns is fundamental to visual education. Art and design education has developed in this tradition and, over a long period of time, teachers have accrued a rich variety of experience and knowledge. The introduction of any new medium must be considered against the background of this tradition. Is there a role for the computer as a medium for art and design in education? Do the characteristics of the primary school microcomputer, the limited colour range, the coarse screen resolution, the shortcoming of input devices, and so on, make it at odds with established aims and values?

We have absorbed the mechanistic devices used in photography, film and television into our visual culture and the same will be true of computer-processed images. Consequently one answer to this question must lie with the fact that the children of today will grow up in a world where there is an increasing development and use of computer technology. As teachers we cannot afford to ignore the implications of this process.

'We tend to forget that images are a means of enlightenment, perception and information, a source of enjoyment yet also an instrument of power and manipulation.'[1]

Computers are already used extensively in the production of television programmes, newspapers, magazines and in product design of all kinds. And, although the capabilities of professional systems are far beyond those of the classroom micro, this kind of computer usage has great importance because of the way that the characteristics of media imagery influence perceptions and representations of the visual world. Professional design also provides an example of the power of computers as a new and unique medium for creative expression and exploration and as a new means of art and design production. Art education's priorities and needs differ from those of commercial media and design, but there is a possibility that significant creative advantages may also be available in an educational context.

Computers are already used extensively in the production of magazines.

A new visual medium

It is here that we become concerned with the special qualities of computers *per se* as providers of a visual and creative medium, and our ability to control and respond to the coloured light and patterns of shape on the screen. The screen image is a powerful and readily attractive one, comparable with film and television, but the computer also has the potential for enabling active and immediate participation by the user in creating or manipulating images and ideas.

Producing images

A computer makes it possible to produce images and designs using a wide range of approaches and various drawing and painting 'tools'; to save them on magnetic disks and to retrieve them and edit them as necessary. These processes may not seem extraordinary at first but if they are compared with those possible with conventional media then something of the

potential of the computer in art education becomes clear, for example:

- Putting different objects into a picture and trying out alternative arrangements and colour schemes is an important part of image-making and learning about and representing the visual world. However, making changes with paint or pencil involves starting again, rubbing out or reworking. Where a design is re-worked there is often some loss of presentation quality and, of course, the previous work is covered over or removed. The computer offers the possibility of making any number of changes without degrading the appearance of the finished product or destroying previous stages.
- Magnetic storage makes it possible to save versions of an image or design. This means that previous stages can be recalled if the work goes wrong and also means that ideas can more readily be compared and discussed.

  Art software generally provides a

substantial collection of 'drawing' and 'painting' aids, including straightforward colour control, different 'brush' sizes, zoom, cut and paste etc. These facilities make the construction of images and designs quicker, easier and less frustrating. With these 'tools' a computer can help shift the emphasis of visual work away from the skills of production and towards a deeper consideration of design and content.

These attributes produce a truly radical medium which is 'tailor-made' for many educational purposes. It is a medium which is far more sympathetic to experiment than conventional art media and one which avoids emphasising technical and presentational shortcomings. In many ways it is more appropriate to children's needs.

Primary art and design

At present, the computer is playing an increasingly important role in secondary education but personal interaction at primary level is also fundamental both to the developing process of becoming critically aware of current and future technology and to the power of images. The computer offers a new vehicle for the development of expression which is highly significant for the development of children at this level. Indeed, the activity of image manipulation in itself appears to be an extremely rich tool in the hands of a young child.

Practical problems

As computers have become easier to control and more readily available in schools, children can more readily participate in this process. However, the use of computers as a visual medium in the primary schools presents many practical problems – not least those of an already overcrowded timetable and scarce resources. Even if sufficient computers are available, we still have to consider how much time can be spared to explore and exploit the visual aspect.

Using computers in the art and design context is largely, though not exclusively, an individual activity and one that can be seen as parallel with those other elements of the curriculum which are dealt with on an individual or small group basis. It seems to be of inestimable value, therefore, to have available powerful software which is easy to use but which presents a varied and rich environment from which to select. The most suitable mode of operation for 'painting' and 'drawing' software involves moving a cursor across the monitor screen controlled by the computer keyboard or any one of a variety of drawing devices. The list of such devices includes a mouse, tracker-ball and various kinds of drawing tablet. There are also many pieces of software which are written for, or can be adapted to work with single switch devices, sound sensors etc.

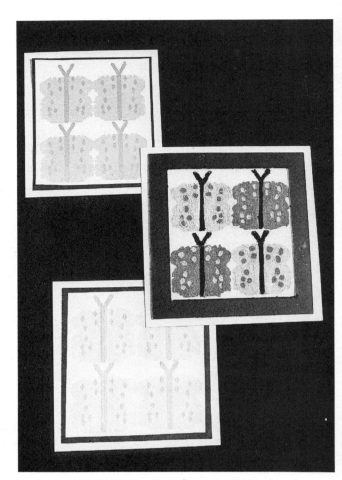

A printout used as a pattern for embroidery.

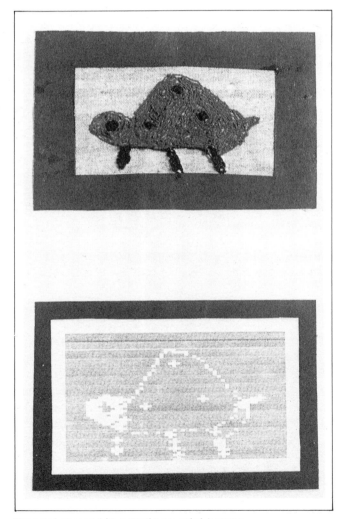

'Image' as used in a topic on mini-beasts.

Advantages

There are many children with various kinds of special needs who benefit enormously from the use of this technology in relation to visual work. This diversity of control devices and the ease of use which they afford have important implications for mainstream children who lack fine motor skills. An important consideration is that these devices can provide a fairly natural 'feel' when drawing. In terms of physical manipulation they do not require much which is different, in most essential respects, to that required to move a pencil or pen. In this way, controlling computer input devices is well within the grasp of the youngest pupil. The only signficant addition is that a given key or button must also be pressed to complete each section of any part of the activity, such as selecting different drawing or painting 'tools' or colours. With well-designed software, this can be very simple in operation.

Art and design software

A large number of such pieces of software are available and a few of them have been extremely successful in an educational context. It is important to note that this type of software is essentially different in use to other kinds which require some knowledge of computer languages. Because of this approach, computer art is more readily accessible for children to explore on their own without the necessity for computer expertise on the part of the teacher. Such software also helps to overcome some of the criticisms and fears of teachers who are not expert computer users.

One example of this type of 'user-friendly' software is *Image* which is widely used in schools and documentation is available from primary teachers who have tested the package and explored its potential. We do not, however, wish to

suggest that this piece of software is more suitable for use in art and design than other similar products, since it seems reasonable to suppose that the many other easy to use software packages would produce broadly similar responses.

Image was designed to be easy to use, and it adopts the approach outlined earlier. Control throughout the entire program is managed with the combination of a movable cursor on the screen and a single button on the mouse, tablet or keyboard.

'The fact that no new language has to be learned and that syntax is made redundant makes the software especially easy for children to control. I found that they themselves explored the menu very competently.'[2]

'I have been impressed with the ease in which the children have used the program. Despite the complexity of it, they have soon found the parts of the program which interest them most. Even those children who have had little experience of computers or have had some difficulty in using them until now have found the program easy to use because of its reliance on a single input device rather than upon a keyboard.'[3]

Making decisions

As the user begins to explore the range of options and combinations that are available with such software, it is clear that a continuous process of decision-making is undertaken, and many of these decisions are aesthetic in nature. The user has the choice of either exploring each facet of the program by experimenting freely, moving from option to option, or attending to features individually. It is possible to look at a particular option and design a specific activity around it which can, if necessary,

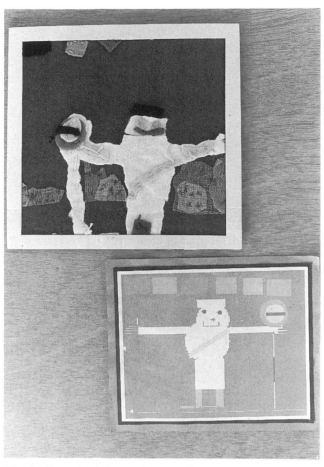

'The Lollipop Lady' – design and fabric picture.

Angela's design was used for weaving.

relate to themes which are being dealt with by the class or group of children. An example of this is a repeating pattern design which can relate well to mathematics, as well as to themes to do with buildings, nature and many other types of work. Pattern work can be undertaken very simply and quickly using a colour fill editor. In *Image* this is know as the 'Mixing Room' but many pieces of software have similar options. They allow blocks of colour to be arranged together to produce extra colours (as in pointillist painting) and patterned 'paint'. The screen can then be filled with this patterned 'paint' in the same way as any single colour and the result will be a regular repeating pattern. The design can then be developed in many ways; by making changes to the arrangement of the coloured blocks; changing the overall colour scheme; or by moving areas of the pattern using the cut and paste facility to produce dropped repeats and so on.

Where do I begin?

Assuming access to suitable software which is easy to use and access to the appropriate computer equipment, how might one begin? The answer to this, of course, depends on personal attitudes and differences in organisation between particular classes. Comments from teachers using such software with their pupils reveal a variety of approaches to this matter, ranging from giving a demonstration of the use of the program in detail to a whole class to letting individuals or groups of children explore it freely on their own and passing their knowledge on to others in the class (a task which in general they are only too keen to carry out). As with most things in art and design, there is no right way to operate such software. The inherent flexibility naturally encourages much discussion and criticism and this can open up many areas of the subject, cross-curricular links and provide a particularly valuable introduction to the use of the computer.

'Would I show a few or all of the children, and should I demonstrate just a few options or all of them? . . . In the end I decided to demonstrate everything to everyone! The reason for this was twofold. Firstly, by showing all of the children I hoped to minimise the possibility of distraction when the program was in use in the room, and secondly, in a mixed ability class I felt that I should not limit them if they were ready and able to explore more.'[4]

'I appreciate the independence this program has given the children and so, I think, do they. After preliminary explanations, I need to give very little extra attention to the children who are working on the computer. This is all to the good in a busy classroom. It allows the computer to fade into the background and become just another tool instead of assuming the prominent position that it does when one needs to give constant help and guidance.'[5]

Exploring capabilities

Early experimentation helps the children to understand and appreciate some of the potential for creating images. The medium is initially and intrinsically attractive; it allows the children to play with the magic of coloured light. It can be a vehicle through which they can be engaged in manipulating images of their own creation, the computer responding to their action in what is in some senses a technically perfect and immediate way. As their hand and eye co-ordination develops they can explore and develop ideas freely and quickly. In these repects the medium is unique and seems to encourage alternative design ideas and decision making at a comparatively rapid rate. A notable response to the speed with which images can be changed, compared with other media, seems to be a quicker appreciation of the design process and an ability to develop ideas in a variety of media.

'Once the computer has been switched on at 9 am, it was rarely switched off before 4.15 pm most days. . . . Most children in the class have enjoyed working with the *Image* disc and the follow up practical activities from their designs. The practical work has ranged from knitting, appliqué, quilting, weaving, screen-printing and stitchcraft.'[6]

Creative techniques

Using a printout

The image on the screen is ephemeral and although designs can be retained on a magnetic disk the possibility of relaying the image to a dot-matrix printer (black and white or colour) adds a further dimension to the work. This is the most immediate and straightforward form of hard copy. All manner of designs can be produced by such a printer and the printouts can form the finished piece of work or can be continued and developed in other materials and crafts. Computer printouts can be drawn and painted on with conventional materials, felt-tipped pens, crayons etc; they can be cut up and used in collages; and computer patterns can be printed directly on to fabric etc. One teacher has commented on this process in detail:

'We have attempted some simple screen-printing by printing out an image. The printouts were used as stencils. From each printout a different combination of shapes was cut. The remaining shape of the first printout was then placed under a silk screen and ink was drawn over it. This was repeated over the fabric. The second print-out was then used to print over the first, this time using different coloured ink.

Likewise, the third was used. The children also did some very simple printing on to fabric by cutting out shapes from their printouts, rolling ink on to them and transferring on to fabric. . . . Some children have cut out stencils and sprayed fabric and paper with dye using a plant sprayer as a diffuser.'[7]

Video images

In addition to the possibilities available with a printer, a video recorder or video camera may be connected to the micro via a video interface. This opens up the possibility of transferring video images on to the computer screen. Many schools now have access to such equipment. This technique adds an extra dimension to the practical work which even very young pupils can do. The images can originate from broadcast television, video recordings or directly from the camera. The technique is highly adaptable and can be used to capture, manipulate and print visual material of many kinds. It can provide records of school events and visits, illustrations for projects etc, and it provides ready access to a more immediate kind of photography and an effective way of exploring subject matter from different viewpoints. Importantly, it

opens up a new and useful avenue towards understanding how photographic images are not always simply 'snaps' but are often carefully constructed and manipulated.

> **my weaving**
> I have been working on the computer and then I did some weaving it looks like the work I did on the computer I some card and some of the card had been cut round the regs edge so I so I can put the wool in the edge then I measured the wools it had to be 60 cms and then you put the wool in the cuts and then you start weaving in and out and I had some nice red and purple and pink and white and black and my weaving measured 64 cms across and going down woods it measured 23 cms and when you go in and out it has to be right or you have to start the line again it was very hard to weaving the purple

Art software is used with many creative techniques.

Further ideas

The nature of the medium itself also acts as a catalyst for ideas. Through its readily available facility for immediate manipulation of colour, shape, pattern and texture, it can act as a stimulus for work in other areas. Video images can act as a starting point for paintings, stories etc. In the same way it is possible to incorporate the computer into broad topic work as a means of investigating and designing.

Most art software can incorporate text in various styles and sizes with computer photographs, paintings or patterns. The use of page make-up software, which combines some of the graphical capabilities of art software with sophisticated text facilities and a word processor, can introduce graphic design into illustrated projects. The computer enables children to work with precision which in turn fosters a better appreciation of the way meanings can be embodied in the presentation of words and images.

Sheer speed seems to be important in

Children can use their own videos with the micro.

this context. The work can progress in a way which corresponds to the rate at which children generate ideas, and it helps facilitate integration between the micro and other media. Children can work in a fluid and open way, moving between the computer and their painting or writing, designing new elements as required. Alternatively, they can use the micro as a visual notebook for final production in more conventional media.

The computer fits into all these processes particularly well because it provides appropriate facilities for capturing, creating and storing images quickly and also because it can provide drawing, writing and editing tools which support later refinement of the images and designs and the addition of text.

'Work need not stop once the computer leaves the room to go elsewhere. My children have now embarked on extension work . . . . Stories, informative and descriptive writing are now in progress. Some are experimenting with painting 'dotty' pictures, copying their digitised images and finding out about pointillism. One girl is making a mobile of the butterflies originally designed for a folder cover; and three more have worked on a fabric collage of the cockatiel. Most of the class have worked on a large fabric wall hanging for our work on the sun. This was first screen printed using four colours and

Patterns for knitting can also be made on-screen.

we plan to embroider and quilt it.'[8]

Other teachers from the same school planned further work:

'One wants to explore geometrical patterns in relation to garden designs – of the type the Tudors were famous for. This links with a visit to Kentwell Hall. Another teacher, making the same visit, is hoping to use the video facility with the children's home made costumes as subject matter.'[9]

Many teachers have commented on the children's development of mathematical ideas, use of language and general confidence.

'To evaluate the . . . program as an Art/ Design package alone would do it an injustice. For the amount of language, mathematical and personal development which evolves through the use of it is immeasurable.'[10]

'Most of all, *Image* has stimulated meaningful discussions between the children. They have talked about the care of disks and other computing equipment, they have advised others and praised their work and they have talked about the reasons why this is an easy program to use. They have discussed their own difficulties and the emotions they feel when things go wrong. One girl confessed that this was the first time she had ever enjoyed using a computer and that before this she had always wanted to cry when it was her turn. They have had discussions about mathematical topics and have shown increased awareness of shape, colour and texture.'[11]

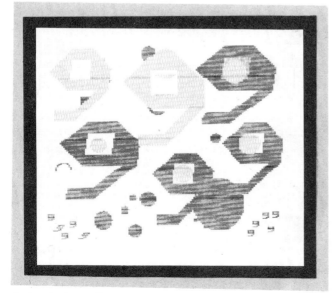

A simple, but effective, application of 'Image'.

The role of the computer

It seems clear that the computer can fulfil an extremely valuable purpose in primary art and design education, despite the inherent limitations of low-cost micros.

Computers offer a unique and exciting visual medium which is in some ways better suited both to art and design and broader educational purposes than traditional media. This is not to say that traditional materials can or should be replaced, but that the use of open-ended and art orientated software in the primary school seems to re-kindle our ideas about how we use traditional visual media. Some of the most fundamental objectives of art and design and general education seem to be made more achievable through the use of this technology. The ease and speed with which design alternatives, compositions, colour schemes etc can be produced are both extremely important in this context. The opportunities that this transformation creates for discussion, decision making and the appreciation and control of visual meaning seem to present the conditions through which deeper levels of work can be undertaken. Thus the computer opens up challenging questions in relation to the adoption of technology in the classroom but it does not undermine established values; rather it focuses the debate on the ways that traditional activities can be complemented and enhanced.

References

All quotations are taken from:
The Image Papers 1987 Ed: Fred Daly and David Spence (Homerton College 1987).
1 – 'Making and understanding Images, Computer generated imagery in Art & Design Education' Prof. Brian Allison.
2, 4, 8 & 9 – 'Image in the Primary School' Linda Goode.
3 & 7 – 'Using Image in the Primary Classroom' Wendy Pearce.
6 & 10 – 'Image and fabrics at Ravenscroft C P School' Gillian Nisbet.
5 & 11 – 'Using Image in the Classroom' Kathryn Gravestock.

The way forward

The way forward

INTRODUCTION

Predicting the future

Predictions are always risky things, and in the field of the development of computers they are especially so. Twenty years ago few people would have confidently predicted the situation that we have now in Britain:

- Britain has a higher proportion of computer-owning homes than any other in the world.
- Cheap, easy to use, powerful microcomputers, some no bigger than a telephone directory are readily available.
- Every school in the country possesses at least one computer, and the majority more than one.

- A substantial number of primary school children routinely experience at school a range of sophisticated uses of the computer, from word-processing to the manipulation of data.

Most people underestimated the pace of developments in these areas, and their predictions of future developments proved too cautious. On the other hand, however, many predictions made 20 years ago have subsequently proved over-ambitious, optimistic or simply off-target. Things which were predicted, but have not yet (and may not ever) come about include:

- Classrooms consisting of ranks of personal computers, one per child, with each child following an individualised programme of instruction, guided and monitored by the computer.

- Books becoming obsolete, their function as stores of information being taken over by computers.
- Most children not needing to go to school, but instead following programmes of study on their own computers in their own homes.
- Computers communicating with us in exactly the same way as a human being, recognising and understanding what we say to them, and responding to us in completely normal-sounding speech.

Given the failures of these predictions from the past, it would be extremely foolhardy to attempt to predict too much for the future now. Yet there clearly are going to be important developments in the educational uses of computers in the near future, and teachers are going to have to prepare for and come to terms with these. Is there any guidance which might be helpful?

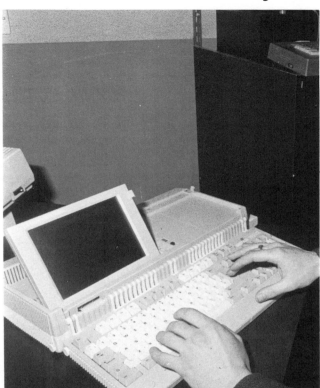

Computers are decreasing in size.

Developments are taking place all the time.

The safest way to proceed would seem to be to look at some developments which are already available, albeit in embryonic forms, and to explore in a fairly cautious way what the implications of these might be. One useful basis for this is to look at some of the new developments in the design and use of computers in the business environment. In the past, several computer developments, for example word-processing, and data-handling, have filtered down from the business world to the primary school, and this process seems to be quite common. For instance, the interest in schools in desk-top publishing comes directly from developments in hardware and software designed for business purposes. There are also, of course, educational developments which have different origins. The use of Logo has a purely educational rationale, and the use of the computer for art and music stems from interest in the creative world. Nevertheless, it is still likely that what the business world has today, schools will have tomorrow, and this will give us some basis for discussing tomorrow's possible developments.

We shall discuss developments under four general headings. We shall look firstly at developments in terms of computer data storage, and then examine changes in the way we might interact with the computer. We shall then look at the possible implications of the decreasing size and portability of computers and finally describe some developments in the end-products of which computers are capable.

Storage

Computers store data, that is, the instructions by which they operate (programs) and the information on which they operate, in two ways. Programs are stored internally, in the memory of the computer. This is called ROM (Read Only Memory) or RAM (Random Access Memory) according to whether the person using the computer can alter it or not. ROM is usually fixed in a silicon chip, and cannot be altered, only read, as the name implies. RAM is more volatile and can be selected from and changed by the user or by the program.

The second way computers store information is externally, on cassettes or, more usually now, on disks. This obviously increases the flexibility of the computer because it does not need to take up valuable internal memory space with information it needs only occasionally. This information is also portable to other computers.

Memory capacity

An important feature of the way computers have developed in the past has been a constant enlargement in the amounts of storage space, both internal and external, with which they are equipped. One of the first popular microcomputers, the Sinclair ZX81, initially came equipped with 1 K of memory. This stands for one kilobyte, which is 1024 tiny pieces of information. If each of these pieces of information were a letter, this would be equivalent to about a third of an A4 page of typing. The ZX81 was subsequently up-graded to have 16 K of memory, and its replacement, the Sinclair Spectrum began with 48 K.

The most popular school computer, the BBC Model B originally had 32 K of memory, and its replacement, the BBC Master, has 128 K. Most modern business computers have at least 512 K of memory, and the new Acorn computer, the Archimedes, has a maximum of four megabytes, or 4000 kilobytes. The growth in memory capacity in the seven years between the ZX81 and the Archimedes has been phenomenal. It can be predicted with some confidence that this growth in capacity will continue, and probably at a similar rate.

What difference does this make? Clearly the larger the memory of the computer, the larger and more complex the programs it can run. Modern programs tend to be large and complex. Most commercial word-processing programs require at least 512 K of memory before they will run, as the number of features they have is vast. Educational programs tend not to be so large, simply because the machines for which they are written have limited memory capacity.

As bigger, more powerful computers find their way into schools, so more powerful programs will appear for them. One of the chief ways this will reveal itself is in the quality of the graphics, or pictures, that the computer is capable of producing. Because of the way the computer produces pictures on the screen, the greater the detail and the larger the range of colours that graphics have, the more memory they require.

When the BBC computer first appeared, it was a significant advance in graphic quality for a microcomputer. Now it has been left far behind by other machines with more memory. The graphics which the new Archimedes is capable of producing are similarly very advanced, and stunning in their detail. It cannot be too long before computers are able to produce graphics which are indistinguishable from those produced by a television, with the added dimension that the user can alter them at will. Educational uses for this capability will certainly emerge.

Along with increases in internal memory, there have also been advances in external storage capacity. The original disks that were used by the BBC computer, and still are in many cases, usually had space for 100 K of information. To give a rough idea of how much this is, 30 A4 pages could probably be stored on one disk. The BBC Master computer can cope with disks with over 600 K of data space (this whole book), while the standard disk size on the Archimedes is 800 K. This is probably about as far as these small floppy disks can go, but other developments are on the way.

It is possible to get, for a steadily decreasing price, hard disk units for most computers used in school. These are sealed units, usually about twice as deep as a standard floppy disk drive for the BBC. Because they are sealed, it is possible to pack the storage space tightly within them; these units typically have from 20 to 40 megabytes of space (from 30 to 60 books!). They will easily hold all the software a class might need, and most of what they produce in terms of writing, pictures, music etc, as well. Furthermore, there would be no floppy disks to lose or damage.

Laser and compact discs

A newer development in data storage uses technology familiar to people who have seen laser disc players, or music compact disc players. Laser and compact discs, as well as storing film and music, can also store digital data which can be read by computers, using a special system called CD-ROM. This system, which is likely to be widely available within the next two years, enables the storage of vast amounts of information, for example the whole of the *Encyclopaedia Britannica* on a single compact disc.

The educational possibilities of this require thought, and certainly imply a whole new set of information access skills which children will need to master. Some people envisage schools becoming repositories of enormous amounts of information, freely available to those with the skills to locate it, which may change the nature of learning within them from instructional to resource-based: that is, from a model in which the central activity is the teacher passing on information to the pupils, to one in which these pupils search for, manipulate and classify information themselves, under the guidance of teachers acting as consultants. Imaginative teachers will find novel ways of exploiting this new access to information. Indeed, there are already schools which would claim to be aiming at this model of education.

Extreme caution is needed, however, in predicting exactly how things will develop in general, although moves away from simple instructional teaching have certainly been discernible in secondary education as a result of the new GCSE examination. These moves ought to come more easily to primary schools, who have for many years used 'project work' as a major vehicle for teaching.

Interaction

Alongside increases in the internal and external storage capacities of computers, and partly made possible by these, have come developments in the ways the user is able to operate and communicate with the computer. The chief impetus for these developments has been the recognition that people who use computers as tools should be able to do what they wish simply and without being hampered by difficulties in understanding how the computer works. This has led to programs and indeed whole operating systems which have been described as 'user-friendly'.

WIMPs

The major development has been in systems possessing what are termed WIMPs (Windows, Icons, Mice, Pointers). The system works on the basis of selection from a range of options represented on the screen by small pictures (icons). For example; to load a file, the user selects a picture of a disk drive; to delete a piece of work, the user selects a picture of a dustbin; to draw a line the user selects a picture of a pencil.

Often the selection of an icon will lead

to a menu of possible actions appearing on the screen, from which the user makes a further selection. These menus appear in what are called 'windows', because they form boxes on the screen, but do not get rid of what was already there. For example; the user may select the disk drive icon. A window appears containing the following options:

- load new file,
- save file,
- open file,
- delete file.

The user selects the desired option and the appropriate action begins.

Selection of icons and options is done by means of a pointer, usually represented by a little arrow, which can be moved around the screen to the correct point.

Using a hand-held mouse.

Movement of the pointer is achieved by the mouse. This is a small box which fits into a hand and is moved around a flat desk area. As it is moved, so the pointer on the screen moves accordingly. The mouse has one or two buttons. When the pointer is in the correct place, a button is pressed, which signals the action to begin.

It can be clearly seen that, by using this system, a user can communicate quite adequately with the computer without having to type in strange commands at the keyboard. The only time the keyboard need be used is to enter data such as numbers, or words for word-processing. Even in word-processing such tasks as selecting blocks of text and moving them to a different place can be done with the mouse.

This simplicity of use of the computer can be exploited very effectively with children. A simple example is the use of the computer as a medium for art. Drawing with the mouse is much simpler than trying to manipulate the cursor keys, and colours and specific shapes can be selected at the touch of a button. It is likely that future educational software will make greater use of the WIMPs system.

Communicating in speech

A further development in interaction with the computer has been on the cards for some time. This involves the use of speech as a means of communicating with the machine. Almost everyone who uses a computer thinks at some time how nice it would be to be able to talk to the computer to tell it what to do, and to have the computer talk back in everyday, easily intelligible language. Computers which do this appear in science fiction, but making them a reality seems to have taken a very long time.

It has taken a long time, of course, because it is an extremely difficult thing to achieve. Getting the computer to produce intelligible speech has now been mastered, and systems to allow this are available for most of the computers in widespread use. Occasionally the computer will 'speak' in a very machine-like way (like a Dalek), but it is usually understandable, and the quality is improving steadily. Simple word-processing programs are available with the option of the computer speaking a child's writing as well as printing it. This, of course, has a magical effect upon children, although this may be largely a question of novelty. Creative teachers will, as always, find further exciting ways of using the speaking computer.

Getting computers to recognise and

respond to human speech has taken much longer. It can be fairly confidently predicted, however, that it is only a matter of time before computers used in homes and schools can do this as a matter of course. The educational potential of this is more difficult to assess. The facility for children to *tell* the computer stories which it subsequently can print out for them sounds exciting, but it is not clear how this would actually work. How would the computer be able to respond to *one* voice in a classroom of 30? Is the process of composing a story in speech the same as doing it on paper, and how might these interact? Again, it is likely that exciting uses for this facility will emerge from classroom practice.

Computers and video

The final development in interaction with the computer is the growing use of video and computer together. Interactive video has been in the educational headlines for some time, and is available now for use in schools, although at a fairly substantial price.

It involves using a video-disc player, which contains sequences of moving images, and linking this to a computer with software to control the order in which these images are presented to the viewer. At a simple level the system allows very powerful direct teaching, matched precisely to the learning process of the user. For example, a video-disc might contain a series of film-clips about particular animals, each accompanied by a sound-track. (Many television documentary programmes might be available in this form.) The computer software could allow the learner to view several of these clips, before asking, on screen, a series of probing questions about them. In response to the answers the learner gives, probably selected from a set of alternatives shown on the screen, the software would then show further clips, either repeating previous ones, or developing particular themes. The possibilities here are endless; this is a very basic use of this equipment, using it as a

souped-up direct teaching machine.

More adventurous uses might encourage more exploration from the learner. Imagine, for example, an adventure game using video. Instead of being given descriptions, or static pictures of locations in an imaginary world, children might be shown moving film, but exactly which sequences would depend on the decisions they make, which have to be made in real time. This kind of exploration might also be more serious than an adventure game. There is already software available which allows children to select particular parts of the country to explore, and which shows them pictures of what they would see there. If they choose to examine particular items in more detail, they can, right down to looking at the exact kind of wild flowers which grow in a particular spot.

Advances in control technology can be expected.

There is little doubt that interactive video has tremendous potential use in schools. What is holding it back are the linked problems of expensive equipment and slow development of software. It is likely, however, that significant developments will take place over the next few years.

Traffic surveys and visits could provide data for the portable computer.

Portable computers

Along with the increasing power of computers has come a steady decrease in their size. Computers that would 20 years ago have filled a room now sit happily on a desk top. However although the size of components decreases inversely to their power, the other parts of the computer system remain fixed in size.

Monitors, printers and keyboards make computers difficult to move around or take outside. More recent developments in the 'super twist' liquid crystal display screen has given computer manufacturers a new dimension, that of the portable computer.

This computer which may be no bigger than a sheet of A4 paper could provide children with a machine that they can use on their desk top, take home with them after school and use when away from school for collecting information from pond dippings, traffic surveys or visits to places

of educational interest.

The models already available differ tremendously in power and price. Some have large LCD displays which tilt up like a normal monitor. They may have their own built in disk drives, or connections which enable data to be transferred to free standing drives. Others come complete with a modem for communicating through the telephone system.

It is quite possible that a specific educational portable or 'lap-top' computer will be developed at a price that will allow every child to be issued with one for use throughout their school career for basic word processing, database and spreadsheet work. Classroom connections would allow children to plug their lap-top into a printer or suitable large computer to store their work.

Lap-tops like the Cambridge Z88 computer are already available and some schools are already exploring their potential. This fully fledged computer, no larger than a sheet of paper, can be used with ordinary batteries and can store several documents which can then be transferred to virtually any other computer or itself connected up to a printer. With computers like these at affordable prices, the possibility of children using a word processor for the major part of their written work becomes a realistic possibility.

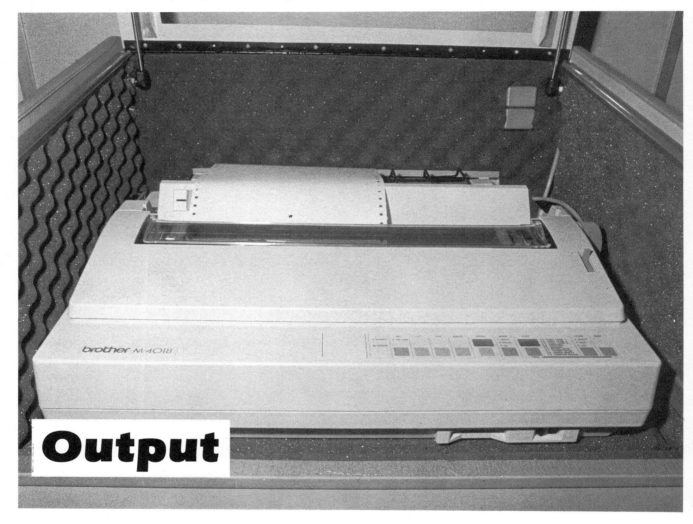

Output

The final area we shall discuss here is that concerning the improvements which have been made in the ways computers can display and output the work they are asked to do.

Computer graphics

Increased memory capacity has meant computers can display graphics on their screens with more detail and a wider range of colours. Computer graphics are already almost as good as good cartoon animation. It will not be too long before they are as good as television pictures. This will mean increased realism in what can be presented to children on the screen. It also has important implications for the use of the computer as a medium for artwork.

Sound output

There have also been vast improvements in the area of sound output. Computers are already in use in the sound production systems of several well-known pop groups, and schools have begun to explore the potential of this medium. Simple computers which allow the user to produce sounds indistinguishable from real violins, guitars, bouzoukis or even symphony orchestras will certainly have a place in the schools in the not-too-distant future.

Computer printout

Improvements have also been made in the quality of computer printouts. The standard printer at present used by most schools is a nine-pin dot matrix machine. This produces its printouts by 'firing' various combinations of nine pins against an inked ribbon, which transfers each pattern to paper. What is produced tends to look a bit 'dotty', and is easily recognised as computer printout. Most printers have a 'Near Letter Quality' (NLQ) mode, which simply involves each letter being printed twice with a slight gap between each printing. This closes up the gaps between the dots, and does produce a better looking printout. Even more recently printers have been produced using 24 instead of nine pins. This naturally increases the detail possible, and these printers are usually called LQ (Letter Quality). Other developments include printers which print in colour, and printers which give good quality printout, but do it much faster, and have easier to use paper-loading mechanisms.

The most recent, and perhaps farthest reaching, development in printing uses a completely different technology. Laser printers are page printers, that is they produce whole pages at one go, rather than line by line. They can produce extremely high quality printout, so good, in fact, that it can hardly be distinguished from type-set material. They can do this for text and graphics alike.

At the moment laser printers are probably too expensive for primary schools to contemplate buying, but inevitably the price will come down. Schools will then, with the appropriate software, be able to produce material which looks just as good as the daily newspaper or a professionally printed book. The effects of this on children's motivation can be imagined.

Conclusion

As noted at the beginning of this chapter, it is difficult to predict what will happen in the future. This chapter has taken a very conservative view of the way the use of the computer in schools is likely to develop. It is perfectly possible, of course, that an unforeseen development will arise which completely transforms the situation. Such things are not unknown. Many primary teachers can remember a time, less than ten years ago, when using a computer in school was science fiction. Schools have not always developed in sensible ways in those ten years, but major advances have still been made. The computer is an established part of the primary school scene, and will surely not go away. It is very clearly up to schools and teachers to take the opportunities it presents, and develop its exciting potential in a whole host of new directions.

Laser Bug program, see page 164

* * LASER BUG PROGRAM * *

Type this program into the computer :

```
1Ø   A = GET - 4Ø
2Ø   ENV. 1, A/2Ø, A, Ø, Ø, A, Ø, Ø, 126, Ø, Ø, -1, 126, Ø
3Ø   SOUND 1, 1, A, 1
4Ø   GOTO 1Ø
```

Notice that to get the = sign in line 1Ø you have to hold the SHIFT key down and then press the ≡ key (next to Ø at the top) at the same time.

After you have checked through for mistakes, type RUN (followed by RETURN) to make it work.

You now have a 'sound organ
Each key you press will make a different sound.
Touch a key and then let it go to hear the sound die away.

TYPING IN A PROGRAM

After typing each line press the RETURN key.

Be careful not to mix up
the number Ø (looks like O on the screen)
with the capital letter O (which is squarer)
or, the number 1 with the letter I.

Use the long space bar at the bottom of the keyboard for gaps. Be careful not to put spaces in by mistake.

If you make a mistake half way through a line you can back up using the DEL key and correct it. But if you have already pressed RETURN just type the line in again.

If you are typing in a long line it might go past the edge of the monitor screen and start a new line by itself. That does not matter. Just press RETURN when you come to the end of the line you are typing as before.

If you have typed in a few lines and then realise one of them was wrong, just type it in again. It does not matter if the lines are in the wrong order. The computer will sort them into the right order for you.

If you have had to make some corrections and want to check how the program looks to the computer type

LIST   (followed by RETURN)

[A mistake which beginners often make is typing 1O (letter) instead of 1Ø (number) for the first line number. If you correct the line by typing it again the computer will still think that there is a line number 1, beginning with the letter O, at the start of the program. To get rid of it just type 1 followed by RETURN]

When you have finished typing in a program, check it, and then type RUN   (followed by RETURN)to make it work.

Laser Bug program, see page 164

IDEAS FOR USING THE LASER BUG PROGRAM

1. On the other side of the universe is the planet KEENOIZ where the LASER BUGS live. Laser Bugs love laser light and when they talk they make laser sounds.

Each key on the computer keyboard is a different Laser Bug's voice. Press some keys and see what their voices sound like.

2. The Laser Bugs are all different. Some are happy. Some are sad. Some are friendly. Some are angry. How would you describe the Laser Bug voices made by these keys?

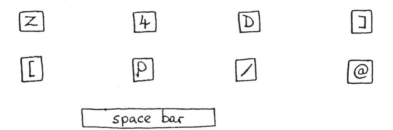

3. Can you find a key which fits each of these types of Laser Bug voices?

Questioning   Cunning   Curious
Chuckling   Giggling   Mocking
Dull and Boring   Excited   Spiteful
Stuttering

© Kevin Jones 1988

4.   Some Laser Bugs are clever and can combine different sounds to make more complicated voices. Try pressing 2 or 3 different keys quickly, one after another, to make new voices like this:

☐4☐ ☐R☐ ☐5☐ ☐R☐

Wait a moment or two and then do the same group again.
Try groups of your own.

5.   Find a Laser Bug sound, or group of sounds, that you like. Can you imagine what the Laser Bug looks like that makes that sound? Draw a picture of it on a large sheet of paper. You can make your Laser Bug as big and as colourful as you like!

6.   Draw a speech bubble coming out of your Laser Bug's mouth.

Can you think of a way to write down the sounds that your Laser Bug makes inside the bubble?

7.   Invent a special alphabet with funny letters and marks of your own so that Laser Bug language can be written down.

Write a letter to your Laser Bug in Laser Bug language.

© Kevin Jones 1988

8. Your Laser Bug is trying to teach you to speak Laser Bug language. Try to copy some of the sounds made by the keys with your own voice.

   ⬚R sounds a bit like laughter, 'Ha, ha, ha, ha!'

   ⬚P sounds a bit like 'Dubbly, dubbly, dubbly, dubbly!'

   Have a Laser Bug conversation with your computer.
   You say something in Laser Bug language then press a few keys to hear the reply.

9. Make up a conversation between Laser Bugs with the help of a friend on another computer.

   Each of you choose just 3 or 4 keys and keep mainly to those. Take it in turns to 'speak' to each other.

10. Work out a simple Laser Bug tune and write down the keys to help you to remember it, like this:

    ⬚3 · ⬚H · ⬚5 · · · ⬚3⬚H⬚5⬚H⬚3 · · ·

    The dots represent 'waits' to keep the music in time.

11.

    The Laser Bugs sometimes get together and form a choir called

    'The Lazy Humm Bugs'

    When you have worked out some simple Laser Bug tunes form a 'computer choir' with your friends. Add your own voices and play and sing all together. Work out a piece in a group.

12. Make up your own words for a Laser Bug song.
When you sing it, you do a line, and then play a line on the computer, taking turns like this:

I'M A LAZY LASER BUG

[T] · [T] · [T] [5] [5] .

SNORE! SNORE! GLUG, GLUG, GLUG.

[7] · [7] · [9] [9] [9] .

Then try to accompany yourself on the computer at the same time as you sing.

13. Copy the Laser Bug sounds on musical instruments. Use percussion like shakers and cymbals.

You can get some interesting Laser Bug sounds using the mouthpiece of a recorder. As you blow use your hand to cover and uncover the end.

Add an instrumental backing to your Laser Bug choir.

14. You can build interesting chains of sounds.
[1][2][3][4][5][6][7] The number keys one after the other sound like a space hopper. Try other chains.

Copy the patterns and make similar ones using xylophones and glockenspiels.

15. How do you think Laser Bugs dance? One of you play the sounds whilst others work out steps for a Laser Bug dance together.

[1] [2] [3] [4] [5]   Clap!

16. Make Laser Bug puppets, or dress yourselves up as Laser Bugs. Make up a play and mime it using the computer to do all of the 'voices'.

© Kevin Jones 1988

Laser Land sounds, see page 165

There are lots of background noises which the Laser Bugs can hear as they travel around their planet.

You can use the computer to make these noises.

1 CRACKLES

Type in this line. Press RETURN when you have finished.

1 SOUND Ø, RND, RND, .1 : G.1

To hear the sound type

G.1   followed by RETURN as before

The sound will go on for ever if you let it. To make it stop press the ESCAPE key (top left-hand side) then type G.1 once more to hear it again.

What do you think it sounds like? It is a sort of crackly, crinkly sound. What other words describe it? You can make up a short poem using words which the sounds bring to mind.

The sound is a bit like crackly paper. Try crinkling different sorts of paper and see which sounds most like the computer. If you have shiny paper or kitchen foil you can hold it in the light as you crinkle it. Look at the crinkly light and shadows.

Where might you hear this sound on the Laser Bug planet? It could be crackling fire near a volcano, or radio signals from space, or Laser Bugs using the laser phone. Draw a picture of where you think it is.

© Kevin Jones 1988

2 BUBBLES

Another line to type in. Press [RETURN] at the end, as before.

2 SOUND 1, RND, RND, .1 : G.2

To hear it type G.2 (followed by [RETURN])
and to stop it press [ESCAPE]

This sounds like water bubbles. Can you think of anything else it might be?

(You could put some water in a tumbler or jar and blow through a straw to make bubbles. If you do this make sure you are a long way from the computer!)

You can copy the sound using wooden xylophones.
Pick out any notes. Play them very quickly but always <u>very softly</u>.

This could be laser bugs taking a dip in a bubbling stream, or a lake. You can make up a piece of laser bubble music using the computer sound, xylophones and water bubbles. Play a bit on the xylophones, start the computer, stop and start the xylophones, add water bubbles, stop the computer, finish with xylophones.

At the same time as you play the piece some of you can blow bubbles using special bubble liquid. Look at the stripey coloured patterns the light makes in the bubbles.

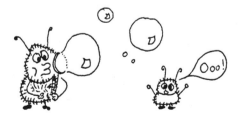

When you have finished with sound 2, if you want to hear sound 1 again type G.1

© Kevin Jones 1988

3 RAINDROPS

Your next sound :

3 SOUND 1, RND, RND, 1 : G.3 ([RETURN])

Type G.3 ([RETURN]) to hear it, [ESCAPE] to stop it.

I think this sounds like laser rain drops.
Every so often an extra big plop occurs.

Copy the sound using metal glockenspiels.
Play any notes.
Make quiet little rain droplets most of the time, and then every so often do an extra loud plop by hitting a note harder.

When it has been dry for a long time the laser bugs do a rain dance to try and make it rain. Some of you play rain music on the glockenspiels and the others make up a laser bug rain dance to fit the music.

At the end of the dance start the computer to make the laser rain drops appear, and all the little laser bugs jump up and down to show how happy they are.

© Kevin Jones 1988

4 WIND AND WAVES

Try this sound

4   SOUND Ø, RND, 4, 1 : G.4

(Type G.4 to hear it, [ESCAPE] to stop it.)

I think this sound is like waves in the laser land sea, or gusts of wind. What do you think it sounds like?

You can make sounds like this yourselves using cymbals (hit with a soft stick) and maraccas, or shakers.

You can make shakers of your own using tins or plastic containers. Put some dry rice or seeds inside and fix the top back on firmly. Shake it gently at first, then make it louder to copy the way the wind whooshes backwards and forwards. It gushes like mad one moment, then hardly moves the next.

Using instruments and computers together, plan out how you can combine these noises with some of the others to make a sound piece which describes a storm, and then play it together.

When you want one of the sounds just type G.1, G.2, G.3 or G.4 followed by [RETURN] to hear it (as long as you typed its line in in the first place!). Press [ESCAPE] to stop a sound. This list will remind you of what they are.

G.1   crackles
G.2   bubbles
G.3   raindrops
G.4   wind and waves

© Kevin Jones 1988

STORY TIME

Now write a story about laser bugs which uses all of these laser land sounds. If some of the sounds give you different ideas use those as well.

As one of you reads the story, someone else can use the computer to make the sound effects in the right place. It will help them if you can write down a list of sounds, and their numbers, in the order they come in the story, so they will have each one ready.

If you are the person doing the computer, type the sound number in ready each time, but do not press RETURN until the story teller points or nods to show where the sound comes when they reach the right place in the story.

The story teller will have to read in a clear, loud voice to be heard if the computer is making sounds at the same time.

You could use two computers.
One for background noises and the other for laser bug voices.

© Kevin Jones 1988

More sounds you can use.

5   SOUND   RND, RND, RND, RND : G.5

6   SOUND 0, RND, RND, 1 : G.6

7   SOUND 1, RND, RND(5), 1 : G.7

8   SOUND RND, -15, 222, .1 : G.8

9   SOUND 0, -15, 5, 255

10   SOUND 1, -15, RND, .1 : G.10

11   SOUND 1, -RND(15), RND, 1 : G.11

To type in a (
Press and hold down the SHIFT key
and press the [(over 8] key at the same time.

To type in a)
do the same with the [) over 9] key.

Appendix

Glossary

Adventure game – a computer game in which the player or players assume the role of characters in an adventure. Knowledge is acquired at random and conjecture and hypothesis determine the route taken through the program.

BASIC – a computer language – Beginners All-purpose Symbolic Instruction Code.

Binary code – a code which uses two symbols, for example representing on, off.

Campus 2000 – an educational database combining Prestel and The Times Network System.

Command – an instruction to the computer to carry out an operation, eg LOAD, RUN.

Concept keyboard.

Concept keyboard – a flat board connected to the computer and made up of touch-sensitive squares, each of which can be programmed to send a message to the computer. Overlays specific to a particular exercise can be created and placed over the keyboard.

Control technology – use of a computer to control a device or system. There are other forms of control technology, eg use of switches.

Cursor – the small line on the screen indicating where the next input will be typed in.

Data management – procedures designed to help the computer organise, search and operate on information stored within its memory.

Database – a collection of stored information (data).

Disk – a flat circular plate used as a storage device for programs and data. Disks can be hard or floppy.

Disk drive – a device into which the disk is inserted in order to read or write the information contained on the disk.

Dot matrix printer – a printer in which the characters are formed by wires striking an inked ribbon.

Dribble file – facility whereby the computer keeps a record of every key press made.

Dynamic turtles – screen images that can be set in motion, given a velocity and heading and left moving.

Edit – to change or improve a program or piece of text by correcting mistakes or rewriting parts of it.

Electronic mail – a communication system whereby messages are sent using computers connected by telephone.

File – a collection of data which has been given a name and stored on a disk.

Floor turtle – a robot to draw on the floor following commands from a computer written in Logo.

Format – (1) the predetermined arrangement of data in a storage unit, eg the tracks and sectors on a disk; (2) the layout of a screen or printed document.

Global variables – numbers, words or lists assigned to particular names and available to all procedures and direct commands by name.

Graphics – a picture, graph or diagram displayed on a screen.

Hardware – the computer, monitor, disk drive, printer, or any item of equipment.

Information technology (IT) – facts or figures or data which are provided through the means of modern electronic technology such as television, telephone and computer.

Input (to procedure) – number or data required by a procedure and supplied to it to operate on.

Input/output device – any device used to put instructions into a computer, eg a mouse, or that receives an output from a computer, eg a printer.

Interface – a device which is placed between the computer and a peripheral unit.

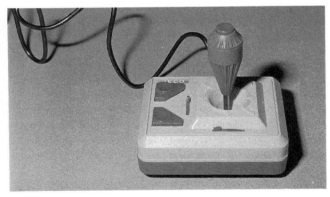

Joystick.

Joystick – a device which plugs into the back of the computer. The user inputs to the computer by moving a lever. A joystick is often used with computer games.

Keyboard – a set of keys as on a typewriter.

List processing – facility of a computer language whereby it can look at and operate on information or commands stored in the form of a list.

Logo – a computer programming language.

Main frame computer – a large type of computer which can store substantial quantities of data and can operate a computer network which can cope with many users at once.

MAPE – Microcomputers and Primary Education, a national organisation representing microcomputer users in primary schools. It produces a regular journal called *MICRO-SCOPE* and holds an annual conference.

Menu – choices printed on the screen and the provision of any easy way to use them.

MEP – Microelectronics Education Programme (now no longer in existence) funded by the Department of Education and Science to act as a support for teachers using microcomputers in schools. Educational software was developed from this programme.

Micro Primer Pack – Educational software developed by MEP to support the government-funded scheme for introducing a microcomputer into every primary school.

Microworld – selection of pre-prepared procedures designed to facilitate the exploration of one area of computer usage or the acquisition and development of a particular skill or concept area.

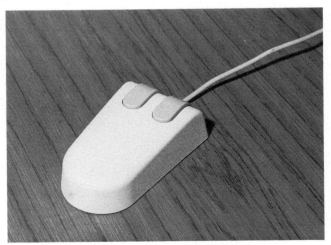

Mouse.

Modem – a device placed between the computer and the telephone line. It converts signals from the computer for transmission down the telephone line, from digital to anologue signals and vice versa.

Monitor – the visual display unit (VDU) and its screen.

Mouse – a free moving hand-held object with buttons on it. The base contains a bearing mechanism that allows the user to roll it across the desk top. When used in conjunction with suitable software, it makes the keyboard obsolete as programs and tasks become completely menu-driven. Courses of action are chosen by moving a mouse-controlled cursor across the screen to a particular item.

Multiple turtles – more than one drawing device available at the same time in some versions of Logo which can be addressed individually (eg TELL 1 FD 50) or collectively (eg TELL ALL RT 90).

On-line – access through a remote terminal to a main frame computer.

Output (from procedure) – information passed from a procedure for use by another procedure or direct command.

Passed parameter – information used by a procedure, stored as a temporary variable that only exists whilst the procedure is running.

Peripheral – a device that can be connected to, and controlled by, a computer, eg a printer.

Prestel – a viewdata service produced by British Telecom available through the telephone network.

Procedure – usually part of a computer program, an ordered set of commands to do a particular task that can be called upon by name at any time.

Program – a set of instructions telling the computer what to do and how to do it.

Pseudo-Logos – computer programs (usually written in BASIC) emulating some of the facilities of the Logo programming language. They are not a full Logo implementation and usually only offer turtle graphics (though some 'Logo-like' programs exist that only offer facilities for computer control or the use of music).

Recursion – facility whereby a procedure may call and use itself (like looking at an image in a mirror in a mirror . . .).

Screen resolution – the accuracy of the picture on the screen.

Simulation – a computer program which represents a real life situation.

Software – all the programs which can be used on a particular computer system.

Sprites – shapes that may be defined by the user and set moving with given velocity and heading across the screen and left running while the program acts on other commands. Usually there are commands to detect collisions on sprites and act as pre-instructed.

Syntax – rules governing the use of a language, including its grammar, how it should be written, punctuation etc.

Telecom Gold – an electronic mail system owned and run by British Telecom.

The Times Network System (TTNS) – a communication system with a central database built up from educational and outside resources, now superseded by Campus 2000.

Touch sensitive screen – a screen which can respond to a finger pointing at a displayed picture.

Turtle graphics – the best known facility of the Logo programming language using a robot to draw on the floor, or a screen image to draw lines on the computer screen following commands.

VDU – visual display unit, a screen on which text and graphics can be displayed. Sometimes also has a keyboard.

Videotext – information services such as teletext and viewdata.

Word processing – using a word processor.

Word processor – a type of computer used for writing, editing and printing text. Software is also available to convert a computer into a word processor.

WYSIWYG – 'What you see is what you get', ie what is printed out is exactly the same as appears on the screen.

Resources

Software

Around The World (CSH Software Ltd, The Town Hall, St Ives, Huntingdon, Cambridgeshire PE17 4AL).

Basic Music Composition (The Tobin Music System) (Helicon Press, Knight Street, Sawbridgeworth, Herts CM21 9AX).

Bees (MEP 'Posing and Solving Problems With a Micro' pack, available through LEAs; also available from ILECC, John Ruskin Street, London SE5 0PQ).

Blocks (MEP 'Primary Maths and Micros' pack, available through LEAs).

Bottles ('Teaching with a Micro: Maths 2'. The Shell Centre, University of Nottingham, Nottingham NG7 2RD).

Bounce (MEP 'Primary Maths and Micros' pack, available through LEAs).

Caving Trip (TREKKASOFT, 10 Broom Close, Belper DE5 2TZ).

Compose ('Teaching with a Micro: Music 1', The Shell Centre, University of Nottingham, Nottingham NG7 2RD).

Cuthbert Catches a Cold (Selective Software, 64 Brooks Road, Street, Somerset BA16 0PP).

Dart (The Advisory Unit, Endymion Road, Hatfield, Herts AL10 8AU).

Dataprobe (Longman Group UK Ltd, Longman Microsoftware Unit, Longman House, Burnt Mill, Harlow, Essex CM20 2JE).

Desert Trek (TREKKASOFT, 10 Broom Close, Belper DE5 2TZ).

Developing Tray (ILECC, John Ruskin Street, London SE5 0PQ).

Dragon World (4mation Educational Resources, Linden Lea, Rock Park, Barnstaple, Devon EX32 9AQ).

Dread Dragon Droom (RESOURCE, Exeter Road, Off Coventry Grove, Doncaster DN2 4PY).

Edfax (Tecmedia Ltd, 5 Granby Street, Loughborough, Leicestershire LE11 3DU).

Edword (Clwyd Technics, Antelope Industrial Estate, Rhydymwyn, Nr Mold, Clywd CH7 5JH).

Extra, Extra (AMX Software, 166/170 Wilderspool Causeway, Warrington WA4 6QA).

Farmer (MEP 'Microprimer' pack, available through LEAs).

Fleet Street Phantom (Sherston Software, Swan Barton, Sherston, Malmesbury, Wilts SN16 0LH).

Flowers of Crystal (4mation Educational Resources, Linden Lea, Rock Park, Barnstaple, Devon EX32 9AQ).

Folio (Tedimen Software, PO Box 23, Southampton, Hants SO9 7BD).

Front Page Extra (MESU Publications 'Learning Geography with Computers' pack, Sir William Lyons Road, Science Park, University of Warwick, Coventry CV4 7EZ, also available from Newman Software, Newman College, Bartley Green, Birmingham B32 3NT).

Gold Dust Island (Jacaranda Wiley, John Wiley and Sons Ltd, Baffins Lane, Chichester, Sussex PO19 1UD).

Granny's Garden (4mation Educational Resources, Linden Lea, Rock Park, Barnstaple, Devon EX32 9AQ).

Grass (MESU Publications 'Learning Geography with Computers' pack, Sir William Lyons Road, Science Park, University of Warwick, Coventry CV4 7EZ, also available from Newman Software, Newman College, Bartley Green, Birmingham B32 3NT).

Halving (MEP 'Primary Maths and Micros' pack, available through LEAs).

Image (Cambridge University Press, The Edinburgh Building, Shaftesbury Road, Cambridge CB2 2RU).

Island Logic: The Music System (System

Applied Technology, Sheaf House, Sheaf Street, Sheffield S1 2BP).

Jungle Journey (TREKKASOFT, 10 Broom Close, Belper DE5 2TZ).

Key (GSN Educational Software, 50 Stamford Street, Ashton Under Lyne, Lancs OL6 6QH).

Little Red Riding Hood (Selective Software, 64 Brooks Road, Street, Somerset BA16 0PP).

Mallory Manor (MEP 'Language Development in the Primary School' pack, available through LEAs).

Mary Rose – The Anatomy of a Tudor Warship 1510–1988 (CSH Software Ltd, The Town Hall, St Ives, Huntingdon, Cambridgeshire PE17 4AL).

Micro Map 1 and 2 (Longman Group UK Ltd, Longman Microsoftware Unit, Longman House, Burnt Mill, Harlow, Essex CM20 2JE).

Microviewdata (Tecmedia Ltd, 5 Granby Street, Loughborough, Leicestershire LE11 3DU).

News Bulletin (Newman Software Ltd, Newman College, Bartley Green, Birmingham B32 3NT).

Nines (MAPE Tape 2, MAPE Information Officer, Newman College, Bartley Green, Birmingham B32 3NT).

Ourfacts (MESU, Sir William Lyons Road, Science Park, University of Warwick, Coventry CV4 7EZ also available from ILECC, John Ruskin Street, London SE5 0PQ).

Patterns (MEP 'Primary Maths and Micros' pack, available through LEAs).

Pip Goes to the Moon (Northern Micromedia, Resources Centre, Coach Lane Campus, Coach Lane, Newcastle Upon Tyne NE7 7XA).

Podd (esm Software, Duke Street, Wisbech, Cambs PE13 2AE).

Polar Traveller (TREKKASOFT, 10 Broom Close, Belper DE5 2TZ).

Quest (AUCBE, The Advisory Unit, Endymion Road, Hatfield, Herts AL10 8AU).

Rally A and B (Longman Group UK Ltd, Longman Microsoftware Unit,

Longman House, Burnt Mill, Harlow, Essex CM20 2JE).

Rescue (Star Devices, distributed by Micro Express (A B Marketing Ltd), Studland Road, Kingsthorpe, Northampton NN2 6NA).

Robin Hood (Nottinghamshire County Council and Micro Express; Micro Express (A B Marketing Ltd), Studland Road, Kingsthorpe, Northampton, NN2 6NA).

Scoop (British Telecom Education Service, PO Box 10, Wetherby, W Yorkshire LS23 7EL).

Slick! A Conservation Game (BP Educational Service, PO Box 5, Wetherby, Yorkshire LS23 7EH).

Sounds Useful (MEDUSA, Bishop Grosseteste College, Newport, Lincoln LN1 3DY).

Space Programme Alpha (CLASS, 2 Howard Court, Howard Road, Cambridge CB5 8RB).

Spirals (ILECC 'MicroSMILE – The first 31' pack, John Ruskin Street, London SE5 0PQ).

Suburban Fox (Ginn and Co, Prebendal House, Parson's Fee, Aylesbury, Bucks HP20 2QX).

Teashop (MEP 'Primary Maths and Micros' pack, available through LEAs).

The Big Calculator (4mation Educational Resources, Lindon Lea, Rock Park, Barnstaple, Devon EX32 9AQ).

Trains (MEP 'Microprimer pack 2', available through LEAs).

Typesetter (Sherston Software, Swan Barton, Sherston, Malmesbury, Wilts SN16 0LH).

Wagons West (Tressell Publications, Lower Ground Floor, 70 Grand Parade, Brighton BN2 2JA).

Yeti Expedition (TREKKASOFT, 10 Broom Close, Belper DE5 2TZ).

7 Days in June (MEDUSA 'Making Connections' pack, Bishop Grosseteste College, Newport, Lincoln LN1 3DY).

1665 – The Great Plague of London (Tressell Publications, Lower Ground Floor, 70 Grand Parade, Brighton BN2 2JA).

Publications

Design and Technology 5–12, Pat Williams and David Jinks (The Falmer Press).

Equal Opportunities and Computer Education in the Primary School, Judith Ellis (Equal Opportunities Commission).

Exploring Music with the BBC Micro and Electron, Kevin Jones (Pitman *op*).

IT Across the Curriculum 3-13 Peter Francis Dunne (Bedfordshire Education Service).

Learning With Logo – Some classroom experiences, Beverly Anderson (Microelectronics Education Programme).

Micro-Explorations 1, Frank Potter and David Wray (eds) (United Kingdom Reading Association).

Micro-Explorations 2, David Wray and Frank Potter (eds) (United Kingdom Reading Association).

Micros in Action in the Classroom (Open University).

Micros in the Primary Classroom, Ron Jones (ed) (Edward Arnold *op*).

Mindstorms: Children, Computers and Powerful Ideas, Seymour Papert (Harvester Press).

New Technology for Better Schools 1987 DES (HMSO London).

Problems and Investigations in the Primary School using the Microcomputer as a Resource, M Hall (Hill MacGibbon).

Reading and the New Technologies, J Ewing (ed) (Heinemann Educational).

The Future of the Microcomputer in Schools, Nick Evans (Macmillan Education Ltd).

The Image Papers 1987, Fred Daly and David Spence (Homerton College).

Young Learners and the Microcomputer, D Chandler (Open University Press).

David Wray

Martin Blows

David Wray, co-general editor and author for this *Teacher Handbook*, is a lecturer in primary education at the University of Exeter. Prior to this he was a lecturer at University College, Cardiff, having taught for several years in primary schools, before moving into teacher education. He has edited two collections about using the micro and reading for the United Kingdom Reading Association, as well as writing several other books and articles, including *Bright Ideas Writing* and *Project Teaching* (*Management Books* series), both published by Scholastic Publications.

Martin Blows, co-general editor and author, is a primary advisor for Dudley with responsibility for information technology. Prior to taking up this post he was head of Race Leys Middle School in Bedworth, Warwickshire. He has written

many articles on the use of computers in schools for *Junior Education* and *Primary Teaching and Micros*. He also contributed the chapter on 'New Technology' for the *Teacher Handbook Maths*, published by Scholastic Publications.

Winnie Wade is a senior lecturer in primary education at Trent Polytechnic, Nottingham, and is involved in both initial and in-service training of teachers. She is part of the primary science team and also has responsibility for primary school industry links. She has taught in primary schools in Leicestershire and South Wales and has written many articles for *Junior Education* and *Primary Teaching and Micros* and regularly reviews software.

Graeme Bassett

Graeme Bassett is headteacher at Wilmcote Church of England Junior and Infant School, Stratford-upon-Avon. He has taught in primary schools in Cambridgeshire, Solihull and Kenilworth, and has led information technology in-service courses for Warwickshire and for the University of Warwick. He compiled the British Rail database on The Times Network System in 1986 and has written articles for *Junior Education*, *Primary Teaching and Micros* and *Teaching Geography* magazines. He has a wide experience of the primary school curriculum and is currently seconded by Warwickshire to work with the county's National Curriculum and Assessment team.

Pauline Bleach has had a wide and varied teaching career, covering 15 years of classroom experience with children ranging in age from two to twelve years. Pauline later took up a research fellowship at the School of Education, Reading University, to examine the contribution that microcomputers could make to children's language development. Her main research was into children's comprehension of non-fiction texts at the point of transition to secondary schools. Her concern with in-service training of teachers in computer literacy has led to her present post of language and information technology consultant with Hampshire Local Education Authority.

Alistair Ross taught in primary schools in London for nine years before joining the School of Teaching Studies at the Polytechnic of North London, where he is course tutor for the BEd (Hons) course. He also directs the Primary Schools and Industry Centre and is editor of *Primary Teaching Studies*.

Chris Robinson

Chris Robinson taught for 14 years in Buckinghamshire. He was deputy head-teacher in a middle school for two years before taking a year's full time secondment on a computer diploma course. Following three years as an advisory teacher in Croydon, he is now a class teacher in South Hampshire and acts as a freelance consultant. He is an active member of the British Logo User Group.

Peter Bowcott graduated from the City of Leeds College of Music in 1984. After studying composition with Charles Rodman Rae he went on to gain an MA in Music Technology from the University of York where he later worked as a researcher. At present he is researching computer-based music teaching aids and their application for exploring musical composition in primary schools under the supervision of Dr Kevin Jones at Trent Polytechnic.

Kevin Jones, currently senior lecturer in creative arts (music) at Trent Polytechnic, holds a PhD for research in computer music from City University, London, and has much experience teaching children of all ages. He has written for a number of publications, including *The Guardian* and *New Scientist*, contributed to radio and television features about computer music, and is author of the book *Exploring Music with the BBC Micro*.

As a composer, his music has been widely performed and broadcast, and he is keen to promote the computer as a useful creative tool in all of the arts.

David Spence was Head of Art at Hatfield School, Hertfordshire, until 1967. Since then has been Senior Lecturer in Art and Design at Homerton College, Cambridge, and has been involved in the initial training of teachers. He has exhibited work at the Fitzwilliam Museum and the Kettles Yard

Winnie Wade, Peter Bowcott and Kevin Jones

Gallery in Cambridge and at the Design Centre in London. As co-author of *Image*, he has worked with primary and secondary teachers on the development and use of computers and software in art and design.

Michael Cooper was an advisory teacher in Kirklees; Head of Art and Design at Shelley High School, Huddersfield, and part-time lecturer at Huddersfield Polytechnic. In 1988 he took up the post of Senior Lecturer: IT in Art and Design Education at Homerton College, Cambridge, and is now involved with software and curriculum development. He has recently completed an *Art and Design Resource Pack for Advisory Teachers of IT* and has organised national in-service training on behalf of MESU.

Index

Acknowledgements

The publishers would like to thank: the children and staff at Moorland Primary School and Marlborough Infants School, Cardiff, for supplying examples of word-processed work; Augustine Wong of St Patrick's RC Primary School, Farnborough for the *Flowers of Crystal* flow chart; Alec Smith of Shipton Bellinger Primary School, Tidworth for the *Robin Hood* case study material; the staff and children at Brinkhill Primary School, Clifton, Nottingham and Holywell Primary School, Loughborough for their help with the music project; Kathryn Gravestock of Beehive Lane CP School, Great Baddow, Gillian Nisbet of Ravenscroft CP School, Clacton-on-Sea and Wendy Pearce of Cherry Tree CP School, Colchester for providing children's work used in the 'Computers for art and design' chapter; the staff and children at the following schools for kindly allowing us to photograph them at work: Wilmcote Church of England Primary School, Wilmcote; Brinkhill Primary School, Clifton, Nottingham; Holywell Primary School, Loughborough; Fairhaven Primary School, Wordsley; and Withymoor Primary School, Quarry Bank. We would also like to thank GA Property Services (Financial Services Division), Leamington Spa and Fast Forward, Leamington Spa.

Other Scholastic books

Management Books

The *Management Books* are designed to help teachers to organise their time, classroom and teaching more efficiently. The books deal with topical issues, such as *Parents and Schools* and organising and planning *Project Teaching*, and are written by authors with lots of practical advice and experiences to share.

Let's Investigate

Let's Investigate is an exciting range of photocopiable maths activity books giving open-ended investigative tasks. The series will complement and extend any existing maths programme. Designed to cover the 6 to 12-year-old age range, these books are ideal for small group or individual work. Each book presents progressively more difficult concepts and many of the activities can be adapted for use throughout the primary school. Detailed teacher's notes outlining the objectives of each photocopiable sheet have been included.

Bright Ideas

The *Bright Ideas* books provide a wealth of resources for busy primary school teachers. There are now more than 20 titles published, providing clearly explained and illustrated ideas on topics ranging from *Writing and Maths Activities* to *Lifesavers* and *Christmas Art and Craft*. Each book contains material which can be photocopied for use in the classroom.

Teacher Handbooks

The *Teacher Handbooks* give an overview of the latest research in primary education, and show how it can be put into practice in the classroom. Covering all the core areas of the curriculum, the *Teacher Handbooks* are indispensable to the new teacher as a source of information and useful to the experienced teacher as a quick reference guide.